T0360964

THE JOURNAL OF
CORPORATE
CITIZENSHIP

Issue 57
March 2015

Theme Issue: **New Business Models for Sustainable Fashion**

Guest Editors:

Esben Rahbek Gjerdrum Pedersen, Copenhagen Business School, Denmark
Miguel Angel Gardetti, The Sustainable Textile Centre, Argentina

ISBN: 978-1-78353-469-2

print ISSN 1470-5001   *online* ISSN 2051-4700
ISBN 978-1-78353-469-2

THE JOURNAL OF CORPORATE CITIZENSHIP

General Editor Professor Malcolm McIntosh,
Bath Spa University, UK

Regional Editor *North America*: Professor Sandra Waddock, Boston College, Carroll School of Management, USA

Publisher Rebecca Macklin, Greenleaf Publishing, UK   **Publisher** Anna Comerford, Greenleaf Publishing, UK

Production Editor Sadie Gornall-Jones, Greenleaf Publishing, UK

CORRESPONDENCE

The Journal of Corporate Citizenship encourages response from its readers to any of the issues raised in the journal. All correspondence is welcomed and should be sent to the General Editor c/o Greenleaf Publishing, Aizlewood's Mill, Nursery St, Sheffield S3 8GG, UK; jcc@greenleaf-publishing.com.

All content should be submitted via **online submission**. For more information see the journal homepage at www.greenleaf-publishing.com/jcc.

Books to be considered for review should be marked for the attention of the Book Review Editor c/o Greenleaf Publishing, Aizlewood's Mill, Nursery St, Sheffield S3 8GG, UK; jcc@greenleaf-publishing.com.

- All articles published in *The Journal of Corporate Citizenship* are assessed by an external panel of business professionals, consultants and academics.

- *The Journal of Corporate Citizenship* is indexed with and included in: **Cabells, EBSCO, ProQuest**, the **Association of Business Schools Academic Journal Guide, ABDC** and **Journalseek.net**. It is monitored by 'Political Science and Government Abstracts' and 'Sociological Abstracts'.

SUBSCRIPTION RATES

The Journal of Corporate Citizenship is a quarterly journal, appearing in March, June, September and December of each year. Cheques should be made payable to Greenleaf Publishing and sent to the address below.

Annual online subscription
Individuals: £80.00/€112.50/US$150.00
Organizations: £540.00/€650.00/US$850.00

Annual print and online subscription
Individuals: £90.00/€120.00/US$160.00
Organizations: £550.00/€672.50/US$860.00

Annual print subscription
Individuals: £80.00/€112.50/US$150.00
Organizations: £180.00/€240.00/US$320.00

The Journal of Corporate Citizenship
Greenleaf Publishing Ltd, Aizlewood's Mill, Nursery Street, Sheffield S3 8GG, UK
Tel: +44 (0)114 282 3475   Fax: +44 (0)114 282 3476   Email: jcc@greenleaf-publishing.com.
Or order from our website: www.greenleaf-publishing.com/jcc.

ADVERTISING

The Journal of Corporate Citizenship will accept a strictly limited amount of display advertising in future issues. It is also possible to book inserts. Suitable material for promotion includes publications, conferences and consulting services. For details on rates and availability, please email jcc@greenleaf-publishing.com.

FSC
www.fsc.org
MIX
Paper from responsible sources
FSC® C013604

Printed in the UK on environmentally friendly, acid-free paper from managed forests by CPI Group (UK) Ltd, Croydon

Editorial

Issue 57 *March 2015*

Malcolm McIntosh

General Editor, Journal of Corporate Citizenship

IN THE RICH ECONOMIES THE ITEMS highest on the list of quick-turnover consumables, apart from food and cleaning products, are telecoms equipment and clothes. All of the articles in this special issue of *JCC* highlight the need for innovation and greater social and environmental responsibility in the design, manufacture, distribution and disposal of clothing and its fellow goods. In the 1960s, older readers might remember, there was a trend towards disposable paper underwear—but it didn't catch on. A bit like wearing a nappy. But reusable nappies and towelling nappies are very popular among responsible parents now. I notice that none of the articles in this special edition of *JCC* is about nappies or paper underwear.

There has been much discussion about responsible supply chain management in the clothing sector for many decades and John Elkington and Julia Hailes published *The Green Consumer Guide* in 1988. It sold one million copies in the UK and was quickly taken up in the US by Alice Tepper Marlin, who published *Shopping for a Better World*. John Elkington, Alice Tepper Marlin and many others have been active in the world of responsible consumption for many decades. In a sense, much of what is now being written highlights the fact that not a great deal of progress has been achieved in the last half-century in spite of the fact that consumption and instant disposal has increased dramatically.

It takes a truly awful event such as the collapse of the Bangladesh garment factory Rana Plaza in 2013 with the deaths of more than 1,100 people to galvanise world opinion. But has a lot changed since then? Many large high/main-street retail outlets now know where what they sell comes from and how much the producers have been paid thanks to the work of people like Marlin and others at Social Accountability International and other supply chain monitoring networks and NGOs. In most cases it was not the companies that have willingly become more open, even though they covertly know what was happening because they had quality not human rights inspectors at all the factories. Many companies only acted when pushed.

The internationally renowned folk singer and political activist

Billy Bragg told the *Financial Times* in 2012 that the 21st century was not the century of ideology but the century of accountability. Let's hope that the development of social media enables the growth of greater transparency and accountability even while it mainly peddles trivia, misinformation and distraction.

The development of enlightened academics engaged in activist scholarly activities is crucial to the lives of millions of clothing and garment workers worldwide for, without informed research, unaccountable corporate interests cannot be confronted. In this way academics are bearing witness to power and lightening the dark.

Malcolm McIntosh
Bath, England
September 2014

DOI: [10.9774/GLEAF.5001.2015.ma.00003]

Introduction*

Issue 57 *March 2015*

Esben Rahbek Gjerdrum Pedersen
Copenhagen Business School, Denmark

Miguel Angel Gardetti
The Sustainable Textile Centre, Argentina

Sustainability (or lack thereof) in the fashion industry

ONE OF THE MOST WIDELY ACCEPTED definitions of sustainable development is the one proposed by the World Commission on Environment and Development (WCED) report— *Our Common Future*—also known as the Brundtland Report, which defines sustainable development as the development model that allows us to meet our present needs, without compromising the ability of future generations to meet their own needs (WCED, 1987:43). The goal of sustainable development is sustainability, which in general can be interpreted as balance between economy, environment and social equity (people, profit, planet) (Doppelt, 2010; Frankel, 1998; Elkington, 1998).

The fashion industry can hardly be said to meet any definitions of sustainable development and sustainability. The social and environmental challenges are legion and concern the entire supply and demand chain.[1] Like most other industries, fashion is characterised by a 'dig it up–use it–throw it away' production system which prevents the achievement of sustainable development in any meaningful way (Wells, 2008). Upstream, the use of water, pesticides and chemicals leave a significant environmental footprint which is topped with repeated incidents of poor health and safety standards and violations of basic labour rights (Pedersen and Gwozdz, 2014). Downstream, the stereotypical fashion consumer has become the epitome of the throwaway culture. For instance, a disturbing amount of garments are discarded after one or only a few washes and almost one third

---

1 Several authors and organisations have analysed textiles and clothing industry impacts. Some of them are Slater (2000), Allwood *et al.* (2006), Fletcher (2008, 2014), UK Department for Environment, Food and Rural Affairs (2008), Ross (2009), Dickson *et al.* (2009), Gwilt and Rissanen (2011), and Bair *et al.* (2014).

---

* Our special thanks to the review panel for their outstanding work. This special issue would not have been possible without their dedication and commitment.

(30%) of people's clothes lie unused in their wardrobes (WRAP, 2012).

In response to the sustainability challenges, a number of fashion companies have recently introduced a variety of social and environmental initiatives, e.g. formulating codes of conduct in the supply chain, introducing take-back systems in retail stores, developing new industry standards, improving company disclosure of societal impacts, forming partnerships with external partners, and experimenting with new materials (Pedersen and Andersen, 2014). While many of these initiatives are sympathetic, innovative and hold real potential for generating social and environmental improvements, they also often lack scale and scope in order to bring about a more fundamental transformation of the fashion industry.

Systemic changes towards a more sustainable fashion industry require collective action by all societal actors (state, market, and civil society), e.g. supportive public policies, new technologies, cultural changes, and consumer action (Johnson and Suskewicz, 2009; Fletcher, 2008). It is beyond the capacity of a single actor to transform the predominant manufacturing methods, supply chains, fashion cycles, consumer/consumption behaviour, and institutional infrastructure.

This special issue has chosen to zoom in on new business models as one component in promoting a more sustainable fashion industry. The business model concept has recently come to the fore as a new, popular metaphor for explaining how companies create, deliver and capture value (Osterwalder and Pigneur, 2010). Historically, the literature that bridges business model and sustainability thinking has been relatively scarce (Stubbs and Cocklin, 2008; Schaltegger et al. 2011). However, recently a number of publications and special issues have explored the intersections between sustainability and business model thinking (see e.g. Bocken et al., 2014; Michelini and Fiorentino, 2012; Yunus et al., 2010). This special issue makes a contribution to this literature by exploring how sustainability can be a driver for exploring new business models within a single industrial setting.

Ultimately, sustainable fashion requires a break with the predominant business models within the fashion industry: systemic changes are not achieved by installing a handful of recycle bins in selected retail stores. Throughout the fashion value chain, there is a need to challenge and rethink predominant approaches to value creation, delivery and capture which currently reproduces unsustainable production and consumption patterns.[2] Rather than perceiving sustainability solely as a compliance and risk management exercise, fashion brands have to recognise the innovative and value-creating potentials of

---

2 In the words of Niinimäki and Hassi (2011, p. 1876): 'Strategic innovations are needed to create a fundamentally different way of doing business...it is not merely about rethinking the fundamentals on the supply side, but also about redesigning the business on the demand side, e.g. in the form of the user experience and rethinking value creation.'

sustainable business models (Nidumolu *et al.*, 2009).

The objective of this special issue is to draw attention to some of the sustainability initiatives which bring hope for a more sustainable fashion future. However, no claim is made that the business models presented will all be mainstreamed and have a lasting impact on the fashion industry. Innovation is always associated with risks and costs, and first-moving pioneers are not always rewarded by the market in the long run (Markides and Geroski, 2004; Simpson *et al.*, 2006). However, the contributions draw attention to some of barriers and potentials for developing sustainable business models experienced by the 'Davids' as well as the 'Goliaths' within the fashion industry (Hockerts and Wüstenhagen, 2010).

At the surface, sustainable fashion may seem an oxymoron (Duska, 2000). The fact that the production and use of fashion garments generate a great amount of waste would make it appear as an impediment for sustainability. Fashion is something that always changes, while its meaning remains unaltered. Fashion—that is a deep cultural expression and aims directly at who we are and how we connect to other people—frequently suggests a passing fad, something transient and superficial. Sustainability, by contrast, has to do with a long-term perspective. But, beyond this contradiction, fashion should not necessarily come into conflict with sustainable principles. Indeed, it plays a role in the promotion and achievement of sustainability, and it may even be a key element in working towards more sustainable ways of living (Walker, 2006).

This special issue

The call for papers for this special issue of *The Journal of Corporate Citizenship* attracted 14 submissions, 9 of which were invited to the second round for full manuscript review. Finally, and with the help of the review panel throughout this process, five top-quality papers and one teaching case were selected which deal with the essential aspects in these areas.

This special issue begins with the paper by Kerli Kant Hvass titled 'Business Model Innovation through Second Hand Retailing: A Fashion Industry Case', which explores how fashion companies can create additional value from the reuse and recycling of their products integrating end-of-life issues into their business model, and it discusses what type of innovation this requires. This paper builds on the current existing business model literature and adds a focus on sustainability and empirical data from two case studies of premium fashion brands. Against this background, the business models innovated with a new focus on reselling their products through second hand retail channels.

Based on data generated in two European research projects, the paper titled 'Quo Vadis Responsible Fashion? Contingencies and Trends Influencing Sustainable Business Models in the Wearing Apparel Sector' by Kudłak, Martinuzzi, Schönherr and Krumay, systematically identifies the environmental and quality-of-jobs issues most affected by the sector, relates them to current and future levels of CSR, and embeds them into the context of important sectoral macro-trends. This paper offers companies insights and orientation about those environmental and quality-of-jobs issues, which can provide a genuine opportunity for creating more sustainable business models.

In turn, in the paper titled 'Apparel Manufacturers and the Business Case for Social Sustainability: 'World Class' CSR and Business Model Innovation', Marsha A. Dickson and Rita K. Chang intend to describe the CSR work being carried out, and to evaluate whether it creates a business case for social sustainability. They interviewed 18 CSR professionals whose companies buy from these manufacturers or whose organisations provide support for leadership activities of these manufacturers and conducted inductive and deductive analyses on the qualitative data.

Following, Elizabeth Morgan, in her paper '"Plan A": Analysing Business Model Innovation for Sustainable Consumption in Mass-Market Clothes Retailing', studies a clothing 'Use Chain' and analyses the clothing initiatives within a well-known corporate responsibility programme from the UK's leading clothing retailer, Marks and Spencer's 'Plan A', in order to assess evidence for business model innovation.

Meanwhile, Ingrid Molderez and Bart Van Elst, in the paper titled 'Barriers towards a Systemic Change in the Clothing Industry: How do Sustainable Fashion Enterprises Influence their Sector?', challenge one of the vital building blocks in the business model canvas (Osterwalder and Pigneur, 2010), i.e. the 'key resources' that fashion enterprises need to be able to create value. The text—inspired

by Hockerts and Wüstenhagen (2010)—discusses the influence of small, sustainable start-ups in market incumbents and emphasises the process of co-evolution.

In the last paper, Kate Kearins developed the teaching case titled 'Miranda Brown Limited and the Passion to Make Fashion Sustainable', which describes the evolution of Miranda Brown Limited, a small New Zealand design brand. This case is interesting since you will be able to consider elements of the business model, evaluate a small business's actions towards sustainability from both a product and process perspective and evaluate the tensions between sustainability and fashion. The subscriber or reader of this journal can ask the publishing house for the relevant teaching note written by the same author.

Bibliography

Allwood, J. M.; Laursen, S. E.; Malvido de Rodríguez, C. and Bocken, N. M. P. (2006) *Well dressed? The present and future sustainability of clothing and textiles in the United Kingdom* (Cambridge, UK: University of Cambridge, Institute for Manufacturing).

Bair, J.; Dickson, M. A. and Miler, D. (2014) *Workers' Rights and Labor Compliance in Global Supply Chains* (New York, USA: Routledge).

Bocken, N. M. P., Short, S. W., Rana, P., and Evans, S. (2014), 'A literature and practice review to develop sustainable business model archetypes', *Journal of Cleaner Production*, Vol. 65 No. 15 February 2014, pp. 42-56.

Dickson, M. A., Loker, S. and Eckman, M. (2009) *Social Responsibility in the Global Apparel Industry* (New York, USA: Fairchild Books).

Doppelt, B. (2010) *Leading Change Toward Sustainability* (Sheffield, UK: Greenleaf Publishing).

Duska, R., (2000), 'Business Ethics: Oxymoron or Good Business?', *Business Ethics Quarterly*, Vol. 10 No. 1, pp. 111-129.

Elkington, J. (1998) *Cannibals with Forks* (Gabriola Islands: New Society Publishers).

Fletcher, K. (2008) *Sustainable Fashion and Textiles—Design Journey* (London, UK: Earthscan).

Fletcher, K. (2014) *Sustainable Fashion and Textiles—Design Journey*, Second Edition (London, UK: Earthscan).

Frankel, C. (1998) *In Earth's Company* (Gabriola Island: New Society Publishers).

Gwilt, A. and Rissanen, T. (2011) *Shaping Sustainable Fashion: Changing the Way we Make and Use Clothes* (London, UK: Earthscan).

Hockerts, K., & Wüstenhagen, R. (2010) 'Greening Goliath versus emerging Davids: Theorizing about the role of incumbents and new entrants in sustainable entrepreneurship', *Journal of Business Venturing*, 25, 481-492.

Johnson, M. W. and Suskewicz, J., (2009), 'How to Jump-Start the Clean-Tech Economy', *Harvard Business Review*, Vol. 87 No. 11, pp. 52-60.

Markides, C. and Geroski, P. A. (2004), 'Racing to be Second: Conquering the Industries of the Future', *Business Strategy Review*, Vol. Winter No. 25-31.

Michelini, L. and Fiorentino, D. (2012), 'New Business Models for Creating Shared Value', *Social Responsibility Journal*, Vol. 8 No. 4, pp. 561-577.

Nidumolu, R., Prahalad, C. K., and Rangaswami, M. R. (2009), 'Why Sustainability is Now the Key Driver of Innovation', *Harvard Business Review*, Vol. 87 No. 9, pp. 56-64.

Niinimäki, K. and Hassi, L. (2011), 'Emerging design strategies in sustainable production and consumption of textiles and clothing', *Journal of Cleaner Production*, 19: 1876-1883.

Osterwalder, A. and Pigneur, Y. (2010) *Business Model Generation* (John Wiley & Sons, Inc., Hoboken, New Jersey).

Pedersen, E. R. G. and Gwozdz, W. (2014), 'From Resistance to Opportunity-Seeking: Strategic Responses to Institutional Pressures for Corporate Social Responsibility in the Nordic Fashion Industry', *Journal of Business Ethics*, Vol. 119 No. 245-264.

Pedersen, E.R.G. and Andersen, K.R. (2014), The Sociolog.dx Experience: A Global Expert Study on Sustainable Fashion, Mistra Future Fashion, http://www.mistrafuturefashion.com/en/publications/Documents/CBS%202014-01-23%20Report%20Project%201.pdf

Ross, R. J. S. (2009) *Slaves to Fashion: Poverty and Abuse in the New Sweatshop* (Ann Arbor, USA: The University of Michigan Press).

Schaltegger, S., Lüdeke-Freund, F., and Hansen, E. G. (2011) *Business Cases for Sustainability and the Role of Business Model Innovation: Developing a Conceptual Framework* (Centre for Sustainability Management, Leuphana Universität Lüneburg).

Simpson, P. M., Siguaw, J. A., and Enz, C. A. (2006), 'Innovation orientation outcomes: The good and the bad', *Journal of Business Research*, Vol. 59 No. 113-1141.

Slater, K. (2000) *Environmental Impact of Textiles: Production, Processes and Protection* (Cambridge, UK: Woodhead Publishing Limited – The Textile Institute).

Stubbs, W. and Cocklin, C. (2008) 'Conceptualizing a "Sustainability Business Model"', *Organization & Environment* 21(2), 103-127.

UK Department for Environment, Food and Rural Affairs (DEFRA) (2008) *Sustainable clothing roadmap briefing note December 2007: sustainability impacts of clothing and current interventions* (London, UK: DEFRA).

Walker, S. (2006) *Sustainable by Design: Explorations in theory and practice* (London, UK: Earthscan).

Wells, P. (2008) 'Alternative business models for a sustainable automotive industry,' in Tukker, A., Charter, M., Vezzoli, C., Stø, E., and Andersen, M. M. (eds), *System Innovation for Sustainability I* (Greenleaf Publishing, Sheffield, UK), pp. 80-98.

WRAP (2012) Valuing our Clothes, Waste & Resources Action Programme (WRAP), www.wrap.org.uk/clothing.

World Commission on Environment and Development (WCED) (1987) *Our Common Future* (Oxford, UK: Oxford University Press).

Yunus, M., Moingeon, B. and Lehmann-Ortega, L. (2010), 'Building social business models: lessons from the Grameen experience', *Long Range Planning*, vol. 43, no. 2, pp. 308-325.

Miguel Angel Gardetti, holder of a degree in Textile Engineering (Universidad Tecnológica Nacional), specialised in shell and crude fibres (linen, jute, hemp, ramie and sisal), has worked in both domestic and foreign industries. He also holds a PhD in Environmental Management (Pacific Western University, CA, USA). Previously he earned two master's degrees: one in Business Administration (Instituto de Altos Estudios Empresariales, IAE - Universidad Austral, Buenos Aires), and the other in Environmental Studies (Universidad de Ciencias Empresariales y Sociales, Buenos Aires). He is the founder of the Sustainable Textile Centre, which he has coordinated since its beginnings. He was guest editor for a special issue of the *Journal of Corporate Citizenship* (UK) 'Textiles, Fashion and Sustainability' (September 2012), and the book on the same topic titled *Sustainability in Fashion and Textiles: Values, Design, Production and Consumption* (March 2013.)

 The Sustainable Textile Centre, Av. San Isidro 4166, Ground Floor 'A', C1429ADP – Buenos Aires, Republic of Argentina

 +54 11 47020242

 mag@ctextilsustentable.org.ar

www.ctextilsustentable.org.ar

Esben Rahbek Gjerdrum Pedersen is Professor (mso) and Centre Director at Copenhagen Business School Centre for Corporate Social Responsibility (cbsCSR). In addition, he is the co-founder of the Governing Responsible Business Research Environment (GRB). His research focuses on sustainable business models, corporate social responsibility (CSR), environmental management, and non-financial performance measurement. The results from his research have been published in a wide range of international journals, including *Journal of Business Ethics, Management Decision, Supply Chain Management, International Journal of Operations and Production Management*, and *Business Strategy and the Environment*. The research has been recognised internationally and has been awarded with the Emerald Literati Network Social Impact Award and the Emerald Literati Network Outstanding Paper Award. Esben is leading a sub-project on new markets and business models as part of the MISTRA Future Fashion initiative (www.mistrafuturefashion.com).

 Copenhagen Business School Centre for Corporate Social Responsibility (cbsCSR), Copenhagen Business School, Porcelaenshaven 18, DK-2000 Frederiksberg, Denmark

 +45 38 15 27 41

erp.ikl@cbs.dk

www.cbs.dk/cbscsr

The Journal of Corporate Citizenship Issue 57 *March 2015*

DOI: [10.9774/GLEAF.5001.2015.ma.00005]

Business Model Innovation through Second Hand Retailing

A Fashion Industry Case*

Kerli Kant Hvass

Copenhagen Business School, Denmark

The issue of business model innovation for sustainability is becoming increasingly relevant for fashion companies. This paper investigates how the resell of a fashion brand's own product can facilitate business model adaption towards sustainability. Based on a single revelatory case study the article highlights a premium fashion brand's endeavours in prolonging their products' life through resell activities and the main issues, challenges and opportunities the brand can encounter in integrating this strategy into its existing business model.

- ● Fashion
- ● Sustainability
- ● Business model
- ● Second hand
- ● Resell
- ● Case study

Kerli Kant Hvass is an industrial PhD fellow at the Center for CSR, Copenhagen Business School (Denmark). After completing her MSc in International Business Economics from Aalborg University, Denmark, she worked with second hand retailing, textile recycling and several sustainable consumption related projects internationally. Her research interests include business model innovation and cross-sectoral partnerships for sustainability and various aspects related to second hand retailing, extended producer responsibility within textiles and circular economy with closed loop supply chains.

✉ Porcelænshaven 18a, 2000 Frederiksberg, Denmark

☏ +45 38 15 32 22

🖥 Kkh.ikl@cbs.dk

* The author would like to thank Filippa K and its informants for sharing their thoughts, internal discussions and documents.

> We stand for Style, Simplicity, Quality. We interpret fashion into wearable, aesthetically balanced pieces, that stand the test of time (Filippa Knutsson, Founder and Co-owner of Filippa K).

THE GLOBAL FASHION BUSINESS IS a vast industry measured by production and consumption. Total annual global consumption of garments amounts to US$1.4 trillion or an estimated 91 billion garments sold (Ellen MacArthur Foundation, 2013). It is also considered a resource intensive industry, with several negative environmental and social impacts along the value chain. These impacts do not occur only during material sourcing and production phases, but also extend to the consumption and disposal phases, which accounts for the largest share of waste in the clothing sector. At the same time, the vast majority of the fashion industry currently operates a linear production model, based on take-make-waste rationale with a large proportion of all items ending in global landfills. It is estimated that across Europe and North America 15 million tons of garments are discarded annually and end up in landfills (Ellen MacArthur Foundation, 2013).

A recent report by WRAP (Buttle *et al.*, 2013) highlights that in the future many retail and consumer-facing brands' traditional business models are vulnerable to rising raw material costs, impacts from growing amounts of waste and developing legislation and therefore need to re-evaluate their business models. It is therefore apparent that in the future business-as-usual is not an option and there is a need to develop practices that integrate products' end-of-life aspects into organisations' business models. It is also argued that when oriented towards sustainability strategies, business models can lead to altered consumption patterns, efficiency gains and consistent system designs (Lüdeke-Freund, 2010). Academic research into business models for sustainability does not have a long history and therefore an overall consolidated perspective on what constitutes a business model for sustainability and how sustainability is operationalised in companies is lacking (Stubbs and Cocklin, 2008; Short *et al.*, 2012; Bocken *et al.*, 2013).

The purpose of this paper is to investigate how a resell of a fashion brand's own product can facilitate business model adaption towards sustainability. Based on a single revelatory case study the article highlights a premium fashion brand's endeavours in prolonging their products' life through resell activities and the main issues, challenges and opportunities the brand can encounter in integrating this strategy into its existing business model. First, a background will be provided in which the post-retail responsibility of garments currently unfolds in the fashion industry. Second, a case study of a leading Scandinavian fashion brand, Filippa K, who has since 2008 engaged with second hand retail of its products and is now in the process of expanding the concept will be presented, followed by a short methodology section. Next, the theoretical framework of business models in the context of sustainability will be introduced, which the case study findings are analysed against. Finally, core findings of the case study will be presented and discussed.

The Journal of Corporate Citizenship Issue **57** *March 2015* © Greenleaf Publishing 2015

Background

The current fashion industry increasingly operates business models based on complex supply chains, extensive use of resources, products' short life-cycles and high volume of fashion consumption, which leaves behind several social and environmental impacts. Against the backdrop of raw material price fluctuations competition for providing newness in fashion is increasing, therefore companies need to rethink their value propositions and find ways for decoupling material resource use from economic growth. Many fashion companies are trying to address these negative impacts by developing their own sustainability guidelines, codes of conduct, implement supply chain and environmental management systems, join voluntary certification systems or multi-stakeholder initiatives (van Bommel, 2011) or enter into a closer dialogue with their consumers about consumption and disposal related issues (Kant Hvass, 2014). Corporate responsibility in value chains is acknowledged by a majority of fashion retailers, but is mainly practised in the upstream aspects of the value chain (Larsson *et al.*, 2013) and even though the garment's consumption and disposal related issues are slowly emerging in fashion companies' agendas, the downstream value chain related issues (i.e. reuse, remanufacturing and end-of-life solutions) have received less attention. Svensson (2007) argues that second-order supply chains, i.e. supply chains that serve second hand markets, are often ignored or are addressed as separate supply chains. The fate of garments after the final sale to consumers has not been an issue for the fashion industry until recently and it has mainly been dependent on consumers' awareness of textiles recyclability, cultural aspects and available infrastructure for textile reuse, recycling and disposal. At the same time, clothing retailers have a significant role to play in relation to influencing and improving consumers' approach to the sustainability of clothing since they are strategically positioned between primary manufacturers and end consumers (Goworek *et al.* 2012). Bringing the fashion industry into the discussion of textile waste and making producers accountable for future disposal of their products changes the logic of clothing production, distribution and sales and extends the activity focus of producers beyond the upstream manufacturing chain to include downstream actions, resource flows and future consumer behaviour (Fletcher and Grose, 2012).

The engagement with reuse and recycling of garments provides several benefits, such as an opportunity to strengthen the relationship with existing customers and to reach new market segments, as an income source through different resell platforms for used garments or new raw material for upcoming collections through closed-loop production (Kant Hvass, 2014). Currently, two broad strategies can be distinguished of how companies address the downstream value chain issues through business model innovation (ibid). First, implementing in-store product take-back schemes for fibre recycling purposes and allowing consumers to drop off their used garments often in exchange for a discount voucher. Such take-back initiatives have recently been implemented by H&M, WEEKDAY, Name It, and PUMA where the reverse logistics system is managed in collaboration with global collection company, I:Collect. While this strategy seems to be a convenient solution for global retailers to set up a take-back scheme, it can create concerns if the rewarding discount voucher is stimulating more consumption rather than guiding consumers in more sustainable choices.

The second broad strategy is developing resell/reuse platforms for prolonging the life of garments and thereby capturing the resell value they offer. Examples of this can be US female brand Eileen Fisher's Green Eileen Initiative, where donated and used Eileen Fisher products are sold in Green Eileen second hand stores together with upcycling workshops for customers, or the Swedish brand, Boomerang, where consumers can donate their used garments in the store, which are resold in Boomerang stores or upcycled into other Boomerang products (Kant Hvass, 2014). Developing new resell/reuse channels is mainly chosen by premium and high fashion brands with higher quality products as this strategy requires the highest quality possible to ensure that garments retain their value and can be re-bought many times (Fletcher and Grose, 2012). This article looks into one of these examples.

Generally, in Western societies, the second hand clothing trade in both domestic and foreign markets is dominated by not-for-profit organisations and textile recycling firms (Hansen, 2004), but over the years other actors have entered the market, such as privately owned consignment and vintage stores, online reselling platforms and clothing libraries. While the history of second hand retailing of clothes dates back centuries, fashion brands' engagement with their used products is a new phenomenon. From a sustainability perspective, reusing a garment as-it-is is considered to bring significant environmental savings and the energy used to collect, sort and resell second hand garments is between 10 to 20 times less than that needed to make a new item (Fletcher, 2008). Reuse should therefore be one of the first steps in a fashion company's strategy to take responsibility for the end-of-life of their products.

Case company Filippa K

Filippa K is a high-quality, leading Swedish fashion brand started by Filippa Knutsson and Patrik Kihlborg in 1993 with the ambition to design, manufacture, communicate and sell fashion with its own timeless style. Filippa K's owners value responsibility with long-term perspectives and the company philosophy is built around core values such as style, simplicity and quality. These values are widely understood and followed across the organisation, which are supported by a corporate culture that cares highly for both people and products.

Filippa K currently operates in 20 markets around the world with seven core markets in Scandinavia and Northern Europe. Retail activities are organised via 50 Filippa K stores and 740 selected retailers served by one distribution centre in Sweden. Turnover of the company is approximately €70 million with the production of 1 million pieces per year. One informant described a conventional

Filippa K customer as, '...not a fashion slave, but someone who is very loyal, has certain values, likes quality and value for money' (informant G).

Filippa Knutsson has described her company with the following words: 'Inspired by my own needs and of those around me, I set out to build a brand that has substance and truth, not dependence on the superficial trends of the fashion industry'. The company's cornerstone is thus being a champion in long-lasting fashion by offering:

▶ Long-lasting products through design and quality

▶ Styles and materials that live for more than one season

▶ Prolonged life-cycle of products through fitting services and repair

▶ All products longer selling opportunity in the store

▶ Second life through reuse and recycling

Filippa K's business model aims to shift from a linear to a circular production model, to eliminate the use of toxic substances and waste throughout the production processes and prolong the life-cycle of their products. These aims are supported by working with reduce, repair, reuse, remake and recycle principles. Instead of fast trends in the fashion industry the consumers' wardrobe needs are in the centre and customers are seen as users and active parts of a garment's life-cycle before being returned back to Filippa K.

Filippa K has worked with environmental and social issues for a long time through their collaboration with Natural Step to develop an environmental policy and their work with Fair Wear Foundation. Since 2009 the work with sustainability transitioned to a holistic sustainability strategy approach and is based on the principle that sustainability needs to be part of all aspects of the organisation and everybody's daily work. Sustainability initiatives are strongly encouraged from bottom-up as well as top-down, and cross-organisational teams are set up for different sustainability projects.

In Filippa K's quest to work with the reuse principle of their products they opened their first second hand store in Stockholm in 2008 in collaboration with a local entrepreneur. The local entrepreneur has successfully run another female consignment store, Judit's Second Hand, in Stockholm. The current Filippa K second hand store sells exclusively Filippa K garments and accessories for females and males and is operated as a consignment store where customers bring back their Filippa K clothes, shoes and accessories for resell. The customer retains the ownership of the product and after the product is sold, the customer receives 50% of the profit. If not sold, the product goes back to the owner or is donated to a charity. In addition, the merchandise is complemented with new sample collections from Filippa K. The aim of the partnership with Judit's Second Hand consignment store has been to learn about the second hand business from an experienced entrepreneur and test the market. Currently, the products can be returned for resell only in the Filippa K second hand store; however, the system is under development where product take-back will most probably happen in all ordinary Filippa K stores. Filippa K is now in the process of analysing the second hand retail business opportunities and expanding the concept. This research captures parts of this process.

Analytical framework

The study is grounded in an analytical framework of business models in the context of sustainability. Several authors have proposed varying definitions and theoretical frameworks to explain business models (see for example works by Osterwalder 2004; Osterwalder *et al.* 2005; Teece 2010; Perkmann and Spicer 2010; Zott *et al.* 2011), yet the term is still vague without a clear and agreed understanding. A study by Lambert and Davidson (2012) of the use of business models in empirical research papers shows three dominant themes: 1) business model as the basis for enterprise classification; 2) business models and enterprise performance; and 3) business model innovation. Osterwalder and Pigneur (2005) have applied a pragmatic perspective to the concept that helps to assist in understanding how a firm does business, for analyses, comparison, performance assessment, management, communication, and to assist firms in their innovation. Furthermore, Osterwalder (2004) has proposed a four-pillar framework for clarifying business models that is additionally broken down into nine building blocks (Table 1). The framework is also known as the Business Model Canvas and it constitutes the essential elements of a company's value creation processes (Osterwalder and Pigneur, 2010).

Table 1 Four pillar template for business models

Source: Osterwalder 2004

Pillars	Building blocks	Description
Product	Value proposition	Overview of products and services and their inherent value a company offers to its customers
Customer interface	Target customer Distribution channel Relationships	Description of segment(s) of customers a company wants to offer value to and means to build a strong relationship with them
Infrastructure management	Value configuration Key capabilities Partnerships	Key activities, internal and external resources that are necessary to create value
Financial aspects	Cost structure Revenue model	The revenue model, the cost structure and the business model's financial sustainability

Research by Boons and Lüdeke-Freund (2013) shows that innovation is a dominant topic in the literature on business models as an important aspect of creating competitive advantage and renewing organisations. At the same time, the authors state that the literature on sustainable innovation is limited due to lack of conceptual consensus. Thus, the current article does not delve deeper into business model innovation literature but instead takes departure from the focus on how a reuse/resell strategy can facilitate business model adaptation for sustainability.

For the analyses of the empirical data of this case study, Osterwalder's (2004) business model framework will be used to analyse the empirical data and investigate how reuse and second hand retail issues are linked to the business model of a fashion company. Even though other conceptualisations of business models for sustainability exist (see references above), Osterwalder's canvas is a systemic and holistic presentation of a business model and its operational approach allows organising and structuring the case study data into meaningful knowledge.

Business models for sustainability

Lüdeke-Freund (2010: 23) describes a sustainable business model as "a business model that creates competitive advantage through superior customer value and contributes to a sustainable development of the company and society". He adds, that innovating business models is increasingly recognised as a key to delivering greater social and environmental sustainability in the industrial system (ibid). While traditional business model research mainly concentrates on the generation and delivery of economic value and value for the customer, sustainability-oriented business model literature suggests that value should be understood in broader terms and value generation needs to be threefold through value for the company, its customers and the wider public (Lüdeke-Freund 2009). Stubbs and Cocklin (2008) add that sustainable business models use both a systems and a firm-level perspective, build on a triple bottom line approach and engage a wide stakeholder group with the aim to reduce the 'ecological footprint' of people and organisations. Additionally, Tukker et al. (2008) argue that business is probably best placed to respond to sustainability challenges via radical innovative products and services and related new business models. Thus, the business model concept is highly relevant in addressing post-retail textile waste issues from a business perspective since the concept is centred on a holistic value proposition (ecological, social and economic value), value creation (seizing new business opportunities, markets and revenue streams) and value capture (earning revenues from the provision of goods and services) by extending beyond the boundaries of traditional firm analyses to include external partners (Bocken et al., 2013).

The integration of sustainability into the business model concept has been studied by various authors, such as Stubbs and Cocklin (2008), Schaltegger and Wagner (2008), Lüdeke-Freund (2009, 2010), Boons and Lüdeke-Freund (2013), Yunus et al. (2010), Short et al. (2012) and Grassl (2012). Although the above-mentioned works are valuable contributions to the field, the research in the context of sustainability is still relatively new and the understanding of what constitutes a business model for sustainability and how sustainability is operationalised in firms is fairly ambiguous (Bocken *et al.* 2013, Stubbs and Cocklin, 2008).

Recent work by Bocken *et al.* (2013) proposes groupings of mechanisms and solutions that contribute to building up the business model for sustainability. Developed from examples of existing and proven innovations for sustainability, they propose eight business model archetypes. Furthermore, inspired by Boons and Lüdeke-Freund (2013), they have grouped the archetypes into technological, social and organisational based on the dominant innovation component, although they are often paired with other innovations. These archetypes are considered to provide assistance in transforming current business models into more sustainable ones, exploring new ways to create and deliver positive sustainable value, stimulate creativity and facilitate innovation. Although each can be applied in isolation, real innovation for sustainability almost certainly demands combinations of archetypes. Bocken *et al.* (2013) furthermore argue that these archetypes are currently disparate silos of research but instead should be linked to business model research.

Figure 1 Sustainable business model archetypes

Source: Bocken *et al.* 2013

Groupings	Technological			Social			Organisational	
Archetypes	Maximise material and energy efficiency	Create value from waste	Substitute with renewables and natural processes	Deliver functionality rather than ownership	Adopt a stewardship role	Encourage sufficiency	Repurpose for society/ environment	Develop scale up solutions
Examples	Low carbon manufacturing/ solutions; Lean manufacturing; Additive manufacturing; De-materialisation (of products/ packaging); Increased functionality (to reduce total number of products required)	Circular economy, closed loop; Cradle-2-Cradle; Industrial symbiosis; Reuse, recycle, re-manufacture; Take back management; Use excess capacity; Sharing assets (shared ownership and collaborative consumption); Extended producer responsibility	Move from non-renewable to renewable energy sources; Solar and wind-power based energy innovations; Zero emissions initiative; Blue Economy; Biomimicry; The Natural step; Slow manufacturing; Green chemistry	Product-oriented PSS-maintenance, extended warrantee; Use oriented PSS-Rental, lease, shared; Result-oriented PSS-Pay per use; Private Finance Initiative (PFI); Design, Build, finance, Operate (DBFO); Chemical Management Services (CMS)	Biodiversity protection; Consumer care-promote consumer health and well-being; Ethical trade (fair trade); Choice editing by retailers; Radical transparency about environmental/ societal impacts; Resource stewardship	Consumer Education (models); communication and awareness; Demand management (including cap & trade); Slow fashion; Product longevity; Premium branding/limited availability; Frugal business; Responsible product distribution/ promotion	Not for profit; Hybrid businesses, Social enterprise (for profit); Alternative ownership: cooperative, mutual, (farmers) collectives; Social and biodiversity regeneration initiatives ('net positive'); Base of pyramid solutions; Localisation; Home based, flexible working	Collaborative approaches (sourcing, production, lobbying); Incubators and Entrepreneur support models; Licensing, Franchising; Open innovation (platforms); Crowd sourcing/ funding; "Patient/slow capital" collaborations

These sustainable business model archetypes provide a valuable perspective to the current case study by bridging Filippa K's business model innovation activities with the sustainability discussion, thus addressing the missing link. Two of the archetypes, 'Create value from waste' and 'Encourage sufficiency', which consider solutions such as reuse, take-back management and product longevity as contributions to building up the business model for sustainability, are closely related to Filippa K's second hand retailing approach.

Methodology

This article is a conceptual discussion based on empirical data gathered from a single revelatory case study (Yin, 2003) of the Scandinavian fashion brand, Filippa K. Often fashion producers and brands are hesitant to allow for in-depth study of their practices; however the author was fortunate to follow a novel and unique innovative process as it evolved. Filippa K is of theoretical interest because they are among the pioneers in the fashion industry that work closely with concepts such as extended product lifespan and timeless design and investigate the integration of second hand retailing into their current business model. While one is often challenged to make generalisations based on a single case study the intention of this article is to initiate a contributing theoretical discussion of business model innovation for post-retail sustainability of fashion and to link that with lessons from an empirical case study.

Twelve in-depth, semi-structured interviews were the primary source of data, which were conducted over the course of 11 months in 2012–2013. The interview participants were selected from all major areas of the company, such as design, retail, merchandising, wholesale, logistics, finance and CSR, in order to understand the second hand retailing from all angles of the company's operations. In addition, an interview with the Filippa K Second Hand store manager was carried out and several in-depth discussions with the corporate responsibility manager, two on-site visits to the existing second hand store, internal document analyses, and one internal seminar focusing on the expansion of the second hand retail concept provided data and input to this study.

A semi-structured interview guide was developed for all interviews to guide the interview questions. The aim of the guide was to aid the interview participants in describing the current company processes and in discussing their experiences, thoughts, expectations and concerns with implementing the second hand concept on a larger scale. The interviews addressed questions regarding risks and challenges associated with creating secondary markets for Filippa K products, which opportunities it offers and what implications it might have on the existing business model.

The interviews lasted one to two hours and were recorded, transcribed and coded using the NVivo software package. The method of analysis was a thematic analysis, which incorporated the deductive *a priori* template of codes approach (King and Horrocks 2010). The coding started with *a priori* themes based on the research interest and theoretical framework (i.e. main business model elements presented in Table 1), which enabled the researcher to organise the text for subsequent interpretations. The *a priori* codes were entered as nodes and the text was coded by matching the nodes with segments of data selected as representative of the node. A summary of the coding results is presented in Table 2 and further discussed in the next section.

Findings and discussion

This section highlights the main findings from Filippa K's process of developing the second hand retail concept expansion to other markets and to integrate the reuse and resell aspects into their current business model. Through interviews and discussions with the informants and participation at the internal meetings, a set of occurring themes and questions arose, which the author has linked to different business model elements. Table 2 is a summary of these findings, which proceeds with a more elaborate discussion of key issues and implications of integrating reuse and resell activities into the existing business model pillars. The discussion is organised around the nine business model pillars and their building blocks; however, many of the emergent themes are discussed as a group because they are interrelated.

Table 2 Analyses of Filippa K second hand retailing data

A priori codes Business model pillars and building blocks	Emergent themes	Examples from the case study
Product/Service		
Value proposition	Long-lasting design Premium quality product Broad assortment that combines recent and old collections Flexible prices Opportunity for consumers to find solution for their unwanted clothes and purchase sustainably Commercial gain for consumer	'Filippa K is not the most edgy fashion, we are not ahead of anyone, we are not the frontrunners of fashion. We choose to make it long-lasting because it is more like our style rather than actual fashion' (Informant J)

Continued

The Journal of Corporate Citizenship Issue 57 *March 2015* © Greenleaf Publishing 2015

A priori codes Business model pillars and building blocks	Emergent themes	Examples from the case study
Customer interface		
Target customer	Loyal customers who value timeless design and quality Broadened customer segments (e.g. price sensitive and eco-minded) Customers as suppliers and co-producers of value	'We have different types of customers and they are mostly women and I think they think its too expensive in the regular shop, but they really like Filippa K but they can't afford it' (Informant B)
Distribution channel	Selection of the proper distribution channel (e.g. store-in-store, stand-alone store, pop-up store) Easy store access and convenience of the resell service Market maturity (brand awareness and second hand shopping behaviour)	'If the stores are run as separate stores, it will provide greater value for each channel to make sure the concept gets best condition. There are different customers and in that way they can provide different types of experience' (Informant F)
Customer relationships	Engaging and effective communication and marketing strategy Customer engagement form (e.g. donation, compensation, consignment contract) Convenient and attractive product take-back and incentive system	'...when you want to create a loyal customer you want to make the service easy' (Informant F) 'It is very important to get the marketing with it, to make it aware to consumers of what we are doing' (Informant F)
Infrastructure management		
Value configuration	Reverse supply chain and its management Know-how of second hand retailing and markets Merchandise management	'I think it's important to have somebody that knows the business in the market you go in, the second hand market' (Informant G) 'The most difficult part is to get the merchandise to come in. You would really have to focus on getting the awareness out' (Informant G)
Key capabilities	Strategic long-term management Personnel training and engagement Supportive organisational culture Cross-organisational collaboration (i.e. business model integration) Organisational learning	'Everything we do is supposed to be part of the business model itself, otherwise it's going to be difficult' (Informant A) '...we all need to learn, it's a completely new field. When you get garments in the store... What different price levels? How do you judge it?' (Informant A)

Continued

A priori codes Business model pillars and building blocks	Emergent themes	Examples from the case study
Partnerships	Partnerships for knowledge and resource sharing (e.g. local charities, local entrepreneurs) Partnership with recycling companies for closed loop solutions Tailor-made set-up for each market if partnering with charities	'...we need to have partners for these garments that we cannot sell in our stores. We can sell it, but in another channel like Red Cross or they can give it away to homeless people' (Informant I) '...we need to find companies that upcycle and reuse...' (Informant F)
Financial aspects		
Revenue streams	Revenue from resell of clothes and collection samples Increased revenue from repeat customers Unified and clear pricing strategy for business and merchandise planning Risk of cannibalisation (especially with store-in-store)	' The interesting thing actually is that the second hand store today is actually making quite good profit so you can do good business with second hand' (Informant A) '...in case of store-in-store concept, there can be cannibal effect. Which one to focus also from the sales personnel perspective?' (Informant F)
Cost structure	Reverse logistics (i.e. collection, sorting, redistribution and pricing) Discount voucher Uncertain sales and revenue forecasts Cost efficiency related to fewer collections	'I guess you have to keep it very local, so that we don't send things back and forth. Suddenly all the transport costs... which are even more than the items themselves' (Informant I)

Product

The central issue of each business model is its value proposition, which consists of five value stages: value creation, value purchase, value use, value renewal and value transfer (Osterwalder, 2004:43). Traditionally, the main value for a fashion customer is the buying experience created during a purchase or use during the actual consumption of a garment. However, the value renewal and value transfer stages can provide additional opportunities for customers. For example, repair of a previously owned garment, wardrobe renewal with used garments from earlier collections or getting rid of garments that have become obsolescent through resell.

Long-lasting design and premium quality product

Filippa K's value proposition is high-quality fashion and long-lasting design, which, based on this case study, can be considered as preconditions for reselling own brand products. The Filippa K second hand store is proof of these preconditions and as one of the informants stated, 'to make a second-hand store with one brand is not easy. But if we can do that, it shows that we are really serious about it. It's really a quality stamp'. Nowadays, a fashion product's life-cycle is shorter than it used to be, often because of decreased quality or constant need for wardrobe renewal. Recent research shows that an estimated lifetime of a garment is 2.2 years or less (Buttle *et al.*, 2013) or even only a couple of uses (Goworek *et al.*, 2012), while earlier studies from Scandinavia refer to 7–8 years (Klepp, 2001). An internal study among Filippa K customers conducted by the brand shows that 74% of their customers keep their products more than 4 years, while for 39% of them it is between 5 and 6 years.

Expanded assortment, price flexibility and solution for unwanted clothes

With the second hand retail channel Filippa K provides customers with additional value propositions, such as greater product diversification with previous collections' style and colours at a more flexible price range. The durability of Filippa K products also indicates that there are garments in people's closets that can complement the supply of the second hand store with a diverse assortment. In addition, the second hand channel offers Filippa K customers a sustainable way for prolonging the life of their unwanted garments or need for wardrobe newness by not producing and selling more new items but reusing more of the existing garments while generating commercial gain through a consignment policy. The reselling alternative may even entice the purchase of first hand garments as customers may see the purchase of a high quality product as an investment which can be resold when no longer needed, in this case merging the first hand and second hand customer groups. Based on an internal customer survey carried out by Filippa K 70% of their existing customers in Sweden have Filippa K garments, shoes or accessories in their wardrobe that they would sell in the second hand store and 87 % would buy second hand Filippa K clothes. This confirms that the customers perceive value in the second hand retailing both by getting rid of their unwanted clothes and renewing their wardrobe with used Filippa K garments. Additional value for customers can also be created from repair services and in-store repair and redesign workshops, which was discussed by several informants. Currently, the idea of redesign has not been implemented, but a repair service is offered for customers to prolong the life of their garments. Studies show that repair of clothes is occasionally used by consumers, especially in the case of expensive clothing and favourite items that have functional, symbolic, aesthetic, and exchange value (Laitala and Boks, 2012). Giving consumers the opportunity to learn how to repair and up-cycle their garments combined with a store event also provides the value of a social gathering.

Customer interface

Based on the case study findings there are three main areas related to customer interface when innovating the business model with a focus on second hand retailing. These are an analysis of how to engage with existing and potentially new customer segments (target customer) and motivating them to return their used clothes and purchase a used product (customer relationship); an analyses of the brand's awareness and market maturity; and finally a selection of the right retail format for the market entry (distribution channel).

Broadened customer segments

Fashion retailers engaging with second hand retailing need to redefine their customer groups. In addition to conventional customers the second hand retail channel tends to attract new customer segments. There are several reasons for second hand shopping, such as availability of unusual items that are often unavailable in a new goods market, visual stimulation and excitement due to the wide variety of goods, the urge to hunt for bargains, and feelings of affiliation and social interaction, as well as motives related to distancing and avoiding the classical market system along with ethical and ecological concerns (Guiot and Roux, 2010). This demonstrates that second hand shoppers' motives are not always entirely economic. There was a wide agreement among informants that the second hand outlet attracts new customers who are more price sensitive or ecologically minded, but also existing customers who are loyal to Filippa K's values and long-lasting design. However, there are also consumers who are negatively minded towards second hand consumption. For years, buying and wearing second hand clothes has had some negative stigmatisation related to hygienic issues, non-trendiness and because it is embarrassing to buy and wear clothes that somebody else has worn before (Ekström et al., 2012). Here lies a vast opportunity for fashion retailers to change these stigmas. Such opportunities include making the store attractive and exclusive, as it is known that consumers patronise stores whose image complements their self-perceptions and unconscious needs, as well as perceptions of the store's quality, the availability of products within the store, the image of the store, and consumers' general emotional reactions toward second hand stores (Darley and Lim, 1999). Making the second hand stores attractive and stylish that reflect Filippa K values was also found to be extremely important by the informants.

Customers as suppliers and co-producers of value

The business model customer interface pillar is directly related to strategic and operational marketing issues and aims to make customers involved and responsible partners in value creation processes (Lüdeke-Freund, 2009) and motivates them to take responsibility for their consumption (Boons and Lüdeke-Freund, 2013). In addition, Sorescu (2011) argues that in many retail environments customers become co-producers of value and this is strongly represented in the case of donation or consignment-based second hand retailing where customers become suppliers of merchandise for the second hand store. One of the biggest concerns expressed by several of the informants was the sourcing of products since the supply of merchandise is a key success factor for a retail store and Filippa K is highly dependent on their current customers to return their unwanted garments. As one of the inform-ants explained: 'Even though there is an increase in acceptance of second hand retailing, there is still the challenge in getting people to bring their clothes'. Therefore, convenience of the take-back service is very important in motivat-ing customers to return their products. In addition, effective marketing and communication strategies are essential in both engaging with consumers to return their clothes as well as to purchase used clothes. Strengthening the customer relationship may happen for example through strategies to reward loyal customers through special sales promotions and exclusive information of new arrivals (Darley and Lim, 1999). Finally, in order to manage the supply risk, other types of merchandise could be distributed via second hand outlets, such as collection samples and leftovers from previous collections. Currently, Filippa K Second Hand is selling both second hand clothes sourced directly from consumers, but also samples of past collections, which is, according to the current second hand store manager, a strong attraction element for cus-tomers. While this acts as an attraction to customers it also helps to increase the sale of second hand garments.

Distribution channel and market maturity

Another critical dimension that the interviews revealed in relation to mer-chandise supply is market maturity. This raised issues related to the number of distribution outlets on the market, the brand's length of presence on the market, reputation and awareness, and whether there are enough garments circulating on the market to meet supply needs. The informants found that for Filippa K to enter a second hand market with certainty requires at least five to six conventional stores per market with at least five to six years of operation.

An additional important question that was raised by the informants was if the second hand retail format should be a store-in-store or stand-alone store. While store-in-store carries lower market entry risks and requires less resources, it can also create a cannibal effect for the conventional store with first hand products. Consequently, if the stores are run as separate entities it will create greater value for each channel and customers are provided with different types of shopping experience. Operating a second hand store also requires a specific know-how of the second hand market and competence in handling the used products (e.g. how to value the used garments) that the store personnel of a conventional store might not have.

Customer engagement form

In addition to convenience and effective communication to find motivated customers to bring back their products and purchase a second hand product, selection of the right engagement form that matches the specific customer segment is essential. Informants discussed two formats, namely consignment store and donation-based store. A consignment store is where customers sell their items based on a consignment contract and the profit is shared once the item is sold. A donation-based store is where customers donate their items for compensation and the retailer becomes an owner of these products. While the consignment store concept is more locally oriented and allows building a closer customer contact, it is also resource intensive and has high transaction costs in the form of item handling, tracking and customer relationship management. The donation-based concept has less customer relationship management and more control over the reverse supply chain since items will be sorted, priced and redistributed centrally. At the same time, the charitable focused format may require more transparency in handling and reselling the clothes as customers may feel that their returned items are worth more than the received voucher or they wish to donate clothes for a social cause and they may not accept the company making a profit on their behalf. Therefore, transparency and clear communication of the environmental and social impacts of the reuse and recycling of the garments, and the overview of the earned and spent funds should be considered.

Infrastructure management

A central part of developing a reuse/resell initiative from an infrastructure management pillar perspective is to analyse a company's current resources and activities, logistical practices and partnerships depending on which new value propositions the company is striving for. One of the key issues for fashion brands that wish to engage with take-back of their products for reuse and recycling purposes is to choose an appropriate reverse supply chain structure that matches the company's needs. While the supply and merchandise management of first hand products are widely practised, a reverse supply chain is often more complex (Kumar and Putnam, 2008).

Reverse supply chain management

The reverse supply chain for the second hand retail concept requires thorough planning and coordination of additional services, such as customer service for product take-back, sorting (sometimes also repairing or washing), pricing, warehousing, transportation and end-of-life management of lower quality items. Furthermore, expanding the second hand concept to different markets might require a tailor-made reverse supply chain that is both economically viable, consumer-convenient and with low environmental impact.

Merchandise management is another field, which requires answers to questions such as: how to ensure a steady supply of merchandise, how to price the items and how to communicate and market the fact that often there is only one item of each garment and in one size. Raghavan (2010) argues that retailers usually do not like product take-backs because of the related storage and transportation costs, but there is an immense opportunity for collaboration with other companies.

Organisational capabilities

The third element of the infrastructure pillar is organisational capabilities, understood in the form of strategic management, organisational learning, and innovation management (Lüdeke-Freund, 2009). Entering the post-retail phase of the product life-cycle requires a strategic direction for sustainability and long-term perspectives of the company, openness towards innovation, experimentation and learning. As discussed above, reverse supply chain and second hand retailing requires new expertise in procurement of stock, handling of used garments, market knowledge of second hand markets, specifics of textile reuse and recycling and finally the job training that justifies and supports the value of reuse. These are all new areas for a conventional fashion retailer and therefore the organisation has to go through an extensive learning process. For the second hand retail initiative to be a success Filippa K tries to integrate it into the company's business model, which requires cross-organisational engagement and representatives from different company functions, such as design, logistics, retailing, marketing, financing, and CSR.

Partnerships

Findings from this case study confirm that for developing a post-retail initiative there is a need for partnerships, knowledge and resource sharing in order to set up a system that supports the supply and distribution of used products, as well as for finding sustainable end-of-life solutions for garments with low resell value. Currently, Filippa K partners with a local entrepreneur who provides daily operation for the second hand store based on her long-term know-how and market experience from the second hand markets. In addition, there are currently partnerships with local charity organisations who are involved with the resell of those collection samples that do not resell in the second hand store. The partnership with local charities allows Filippa K to build a connection with the local community, which allows the company to capture the value of used garments locally as long as possible before transporting garments to international recycling markets. However, charity organisations operate with different business models in different markets and therefore a tailor-made setup for each market is required, which can be resource intensive and requires local coordination. Additionally, Filippa K is in collaboration with recycling companies in order to find final end-of-life solutions for their garments.

Finally, setting up a product take-back system needs to also involve other distributors, such as wholesalers and franchise stores, and therefore a partnership agreement should be expanded with post-retail issues that motivates distributors to provide product collection services in their stores. This may add additional cost, which was addressed by one informant:

some would understand and support the concept, but there are not many as I think they would say ok, that is a very good thing for the sustainability but if we lose money? So, we need to take the cost for that (Informant L).

Financial aspects

Revenue streams

This business model pillar refers to questions such as what new revenue streams can resell activities bring and what costs and other financial risks are related to it. Earlier research has argued that second hand retailing reduces a substantial proportion of conventional retailers' revenues (Guiot and Roux, 2010). However, findings from the Filippa K case study indicate that second hand retailing has the potential for financial value for conventional retailers through increased customer base, increased customer loyalty since customers have to come back with the used products, income generated from the resell of clothes and finding a sales channel for collection samples. Currently, the Filippa K Second Hand store generates a stable profit and is proof of its economic viability. Several informants acknowledged that they see a business opportunity behind the idea, as one informant stated,

> We see it as an opportunity because we know that our clothing can really stand the test of time, so we can actually get more customers, we don't want each customer to buy more or faster, but we can have new customers (Informant A).

Or expressed by another informant:

> I would say it's doing the right thing for Filippa K and doing the right thing would, in the end, mean that we actually earn more money. Because it's part of us, and with doing fashion that's long-lasting, that is what Filippa Knutsson said from the beginning when she started, so it's a part of our nature actually (Informant K).

A study by WRAP (Buttle et al., 2013) on the financial viability and resource implications for new business models in the clothing sector also suggests that retailers offering a resale channel for their garments is one of the most commercially viable models over the long and short term.

Cost structure

While it is argued that the resell of fashion is a commercially viable model, there are still costs that must be considered. The main reoccurring cost issue discussed by informants was reverse logistics, i.e. costs related to collection, handling, sorting and redistribution. For example, if the product can be handed-in in all regular stores the logistics costs are incurred at two points, through the transportation of the garment from collection points to the central processing warehouse, and after sorting and processing, to transport them back to second hand retail stores (Buttle et al., 2013). Another issue with reverse logistics is the need for keeping the redistribution as local as possible, both for keeping the costs down as well as not creating an additional environmental impact.

Finally, applying the consignment based system requires sharing the profit with the owner of the garment, where the market practice is an equal share or a 60-40 split with the larger share going to the retailer, while the donation-voucher model brings along costs related to a voucher system and providing every customer a discount on a new purchase.

Conclusion

Until recently, fashion companies' main focus was on creating and capturing value from the sale of new products, and once the garments were sold these products were not regarded as part of their business model. However, resell can provide additional value creation opportunities. This research is a first step in conceptualising second hand retailing from a business model perspective. The aim of this paper is to provide a framework for better understanding of how to link reuse and resell issues of garments into fashion companies' business models. The Filippa K second hand case study was analysed in relation to the business model framework, which shows that creating value from waste and encouraging sufficiency through reuse and resell can facilitate new value propositions and business model innovation towards sustainability.

The study unfolded several issues that are relevant for the company to address when engaging with the post-retail phase of their products and integrating reselling activities into their current business model. A framework for understanding second hand retail development from a holistic business model perspective was proposed and a set of provisions that are necessary for fashion brands to integrate the resell activity into their current business model was suggested.

The findings suggest that there is a potential for fashion brands with premium quality products to integrate resell activities into their current business models and value propositions. Furthermore, the study demonstrates that resell activities bring additional value to the fashion company, as it allows it to build closer relationship with customers, attract additional customer groups and generate income with used products or collection samples. However, several prerequisites have to be in place, such as a product's high quality, strong brand awareness and market maturity. In addition, redefinition of customer groups and new ways of customer engagement are required since customers become suppliers of merchandise in the context of second hand retailing. The study also reveals that the main challenge with second hand retailing is related to reverse logistics and setting up a collection and redistribution system that is convenient, cost-effective and matches the needs of each market.

The main limitation of this paper is a single case study; however, the proposed framework may have transferability to other fashion brands who are willing to take a wider responsibility for their products and prolong their products' lifecycle through resell. Especially premium quality brands with a focus on timeless design might find these case study findings useful. Addressing these issues can guide companies through the process of identifying reuse and resell value of their products as part of their business model and not just an add-on campaign. While engaging with take-back and resell of used products is a novel activity for a fashion company, it raises a question of how much change in the existing business model does this activity actually require. Does it require radical changes or just incremental adjustments in some of the business model elements? This is an interesting area for further research that was out of the scope of this research article. The author hopes that this paper will encourage researchers to further examine business model innovation which links to products' life-cycles and end-of-life issues in order to find sustainable solutions for the waste and unsustainable consumption and disposal issues in the future.

References

Bocken, N., Short, S.W., Rana, P. & Evans, S. (2014), 'A literature and practice review to develop sustainable business model archetypes', Journal of Cleaner Production, vol 65, pp. 42-56.

Boons, F. & Lüdeke-Freund, F. (2013), 'Business models for sustainable innovation: state-of-the-art and steps towards a research agenda', Journal of Cleaner Production, vol 45, pp. 9-19.

Buttle, M., Vyas, D. and Spinks, C. (2013), Evaluating the financial viability and resource implications for new business models in the clothing sector, WRAP.

Darley, W.K. & Lim, J. (1999), 'Effects of store image and attitude toward secondhand stores on shopping frequency and distance traveled', International Journal of Retail & Distribution Management, vol. 27, no. 8, pp. 311-318.

Ekström, K.M., Gustafsson, E., Hjelmgren, D. & Salomonson, N. (2012), 'Mot en mer hållbar konsumtion: en studie om konsumenters anskaffning och avyttring av kläder', Högskolan i Borås.

Ellen MacArthur Foundation (2013), Towards the Circular Economy. Opportunities for the Consumer Goods Sector, Ellen MacArthur Foundation.

Fletcher, K. (2008), Sustainable fashion and textiles: design journeys, Earthscan. James & James.

Fletcher, K. and Grose, L. (2012), Fashion and Sustainability: Design for Change, Laurence King Publishers.

Goworek, H., Fisher, T., Cooper, T., Woodward, S. and Hiller, A. (2012), 'The sustainable clothing market: an evaluation of potential strategies for UK retailers', International Journal of Retail & Distribution Management, vol. 40, no. 12, pp. 935-955.

Grassl, W. (2012), 'Business Models of Social Enterprise: A Design Approach to Hybridity', ACRN Journal of Social Entrepreneurship Perspectives, vol. 1, no. 1.

Guiot, D. & Roux, D. (2010), 'A Second-hand Shoppers' Motivation Scale: Antecedents, Consequences, and Implications for Retailers', Journal of Retailing, vol. 86, no. 4, pp. 355-371.

Hansen, K.T. (2004), 'Helping or hindering? Controversies around the international second-hand clothing trade', Anthropology Today, vol. 20, no. 4, pp. 3-9.

Kant Hvass, K. (2014), 'Post-retail Responsibility of Garments - A fashion industry's perspective', Journal of Fashion Marketing and Management, vol. 18, no. 4, pp. 413-430

The Journal of Corporate Citizenship Issue 57 *March 2015* © Greenleaf Publishing 2015

King, N. and Horrocks, C. (2010), Interviews in qualitative research, SAGE Publications Limited.

Klepp, I.G. (2001), 'Hvorfor går klær ut av bruk', Avhending sett i forhold til kvinners klesvaner lysaker, SIFO Rapport, no. 3-2001.

Kumar, S. and Putnam, V. (2008), 'Cradle to cradle: Reverse logistics strategies and opportunities across three industry sectors', International Journal of Production Economics, vol. 115, no. 2, pp. 305-315.

Laitala, K. and Boks, C. (2012), 'Sustainable clothing design: use matters', Journal of Design Research, vol. 10, no. 1, pp. 121-139.

Lambert, S.C. and Davidson, R.A. (2012), 'Applications of the business model in studies of enterprise success, innovation and classification: An analysis of empirical research from 1996 to 2010', European Management Journal, vol 31, no. 6, pp.668-681.

Larsson, A., Buhr, K. and Mark-Herbert, C. (2013), 'Corporate responsibility in the garment industry: Towards shared value' in Sustainability in Fashion and Textiles. Values, Design, Production and Consumption, eds. Gardetti, M.A and Torres, L.A., Greenleaf Publishing Limited, Sheffield UK, pp. 262-276.

Lüdeke-Freund, F. (2009), Business Model Concepts in Corporate Sustainability Contexts. From Rhetoric to a Generic Template for Business Models for Sustainability, Lüneburg, Centre for Sustainability Management.

Lüdeke-Freund, F. (2010), 'Towards a Conceptual Framework of Business Models for Sustainability', ERSCP-EMSU Conference 2010 - Knowledge Collaboration and Learning for Sustainable Innovation. Centre for Sustainability Management (CSM), Leuphana University of Lüneburg.

Osterwalder, A. (2004), 'The business model ontology: A proposition in a design science approach', Institut d'Informatique et Organisation.Lausanne, Switzerland, University of Lausanne, Ecole des Hautes Etudes Commerciales HEC.

Osterwalder, A. and Pigneur, Y. (2010), Business model generation: a handbook for visionaries, game changers, and challengers, John Wiley & Sons.

Osterwalder, A., Pigneur, Y. and Tucci, C.L. (2005), 'Clarifying business models: Origins, present, and future of the concept', Communications of the Association for Information Systems, vol. 16, no. 1, pp. 1-25.

Perkmann, M. and Spicer, A. (2010), 'What are business models? Developing a theory of performative representations', Nelson Phillips, Graham Sewell, Dorothy Griffiths (eds.), in Technology and Organization: Essays in Honour of Joan Woodward (Research in the Sociology of Organizations, Volume 29), Emerald Group Publishing Limited, pp. 265-275.

Raghavan, S. (2010), 'Don't throw it away: the corporate role in product disposition', Journal of Business Strategy, vol. 31, no. 3, pp. 50-55.

Schaltegger, S. and Wagner, M. (2008), 'Managing the business case for sustainability', EMAN-EU 2008 Conference, pp 7.

Short, S., Rana, P., Bocken, N. and Evans, S. (2012), 'Embedding sustainability in business modelling through multi-stakeholder value innovation', APMS 2012 International Conference on Advances in Production Management Systems, 24-26 September, Greece.

Sorescu, A., Frambach, R.T., Singh, J., Rangaswamy, A. and Bridges, C. (2011), 'Innovations in retail business models', Journal of Retailing, vol. 87, pp. S3-S16.

Stubbs, W. and Cocklin, C. (2008), 'Conceptualizing a "sustainability business model"', Organization & Environment, vol. 21, no. 2, pp. 103-127.

Svensson, G. (2007), 'Aspects of sustainable supply chain management (SSCM): conceptual framework and empirical example', Supply Chain Management: An International Journal, vol. 12, no. 4, pp. 262-266.

Teece, D.J. (2010), 'Business models, business strategy and innovation', Long Range Planning, vol. 43, no. 2, pp. 172-194.

van Bommel, H.W.M. (2011), 'A conceptual framework for analyzing sustainability strategies in industrial supply networks from an innovation perspective', Journal of Cleaner Production, vol. 19, no. 8, pp. 895-904.

Yin, R.K. (2003), Case Study Research. Design and Methods, third edition, SAGE Publications, Thousand Oaks, CA.

Yunus, M., Moingeon, B. and Lehmann-Ortega, L. (2010), 'Building social business models: lessons from the Grameen experience', Long Range Planning, vol. 43, no. 2, pp. 308-325.

Zott, C., Amit, R. and Massa, L. (2011), 'The business model: recent developments and future research', Journal of Management, vol. 37, no. 4, pp. 1019-1042.

DOI: [10.9774/GLEAF.5001.2015.ma.00006]

Quo Vadis Responsible Fashion?

Contingencies and Trends Influencing Sustainable Business Models in the Wearing Apparel Sector*

R. Kudłak
Adam Mickiewicz University, Poland

A. Martinuzzi, N. Schönherr and B. Krumay
Vienna University of Economics and Business, Austria

Currently, the wearing apparel sector is relatively under-investigated in terms of sustainable business models. At the same time, the sector has been increasingly scrutinised regarding its effects on the natural environment and quality of jobs issues related to its operations, manufacturing processes, and its global supply chains. Based on data generated in two European research projects, our paper systematically identifies the environmental and quality of jobs issues most affected by the sector, relates them to current and future levels of CSR, and embeds them into the context of important sectoral macro-trends. By doing so, our paper offers insights and orientation for companies in regards to those environmental and quality of jobs issues, which may provide a genuine opportunity for creating more sustainable business models. Understanding these concerns and upcoming trends could give them a unique position for differentiating their business models.

- Sustainable business models
- Wearing apparel
- Trends
- Future
- Contingencies
- CSR
- Competitive advantage

Robert Kudłak holds a doctoral degree in economic geography from Adam Mickiewicz University. From 2010 to 2014 he was a research fellow at the Research Institute for Managing Sustainability at Vienna University of Economics and Business involved in the FP7 'IMPACT' project. Research areas are corporate social responsibility, environmental and societal impacts of CSR, and institutional theory.

✉ Institute of Socio-Economic Geography and Spatial Management, Adam Mickiewicz University, Dzięgielowa 27, 61-680 Poznań, Poland

🖥 rkudlak@amu.edu.pl

* The authors would like to thank Regine Barth and her team at Oeko-Institute as co-ordinator of the IMPACT project (grant agreement no.: 244618, for details see www.CSR-IMPACT.eu) and all other consortium partners for the good collaboration during the last three years; the participants of our expert panel for their time allocated and willingness to share their expertise; Tom Dodd from DG Enterprise and Industry for the fruitful collaboration in the 'Responsible Competitiveness Project'; and the Austrian National Bank for funding project number 13175, which helped us to conceptualise this paper.

André Martinuzzi (PD Dr) is head of the Institute for Managing Sustainability and associate professor at Vienna University of Economics and Business. He has a postdoctoral lecture qualification (venia docendi) in Environmental Management and Sustainable Development Policy. He has co-ordinated projects in the EU Framework Programme, has conducted tendered research projects on behalf of six different EU DGs, Eurostat, the UN Development Programme and for several national ministries. His main areas of research are corporate sustainability, sustainable development policies, impact assessment, and knowledge brokerage.

✉ Institute for Managing Sustainability, Vienna University of Economics and Business, Building D1, 2nd Floor, Welthandelsplatz 1, A-1020 Vienna, Austria

🖥 andre.martinuzzi@wu.ac.at

Norma Schönherr is a research fellow and project manager at the Institute for Managing Sustainability at Vienna University of Economics and Business. She manages the EU-funded research project 'GLOBAL VALUE', which involves substantial work on societal impacts of the apparel and footwear sector in developing countries. Her main academic interests are in the fields of CSR, sustainability governance and corporate impacts on global sustainable development.

✉ Institute for Managing Sustainability, Vienna University of Economics and Business, Building D1, 2nd Floor, Welthandelsplatz 1, A-1020 Vienna, Austria

🖥 Norma.schoenherr@wu.ac.at

Barbara Krumay is a research assistant at the Department of Information Systems and Operations at Vienna University of Economics and Business. She holds a Doctoral degree in Business Informatics. Her expertise combines scientific research and long-term consulting experience in business. Hence, she has investigated impacts from both the firm and individual level. Currently, her reserach focuses on the role of information systems on stakeholder involvement and the integration of ICT-related issues into a holistic approach to CSR as well as ICT-support for measuring and managing impacts.

✉ Institute for Information Management and Control, Vienna University of Economics and Business, Building D2, Entrance C, Welthandelsplatz 1, A-1020 Vienna, Austria

🖥 bkrumay@wu.ac.at

O N 24 APRIL 2013, THE Savar building, an eight-story commercial building, collapsed at Rana Plaza in Dhaka, the capital of Bangladesh. The search for the dead ended on 13 May with the death toll of 1,129. It is considered to be the deadliest accident in the history of the wearing apparel sector. Although not the first event of its kind, its sheer dimension drew global attention and made the consequences of current practices in the whole textile industry alarmingly clear to consumers in the Western world (ILO, 2013). At the same time, the accident illustrates the need for more sustainable business models in the textile industry at large, as well as within its global supply chains (cf. Dickson *et al.*, 2012).

The Rana Plaza incident and similar examples show the significant social and environmental issues the sector faces, including increasingly pressing criticism of inhumane labour conditions in 'sweat shops', chemical pollution, and water consumption. At the same time, the sector has been subject to immense international competitive pressures. Particularly, large companies in the sector are coming under increasing pressure to account for their impacts on the environment and society, to assume responsibility for these impacts, and to ultimately rethink their business models (Dickson *et al.*, 2012).

As a consequence of the ever growing globalisation process, relocation of manufacturing sites to low income countries, the European textile industry has been experiencing a tremendous transformation over the last decades—moving into niche markets and industrial textiles and away from wearing apparel (Jones and Hayes, 2004; Taplin and Winterton, 2004). Nevertheless, wearing apparel remains an important industry in Europe. It contributes about 46% of employment and 35% of value added in the sector (Eurostat, 2009). The industry employs approximately 1.06 million people in more than 129,400 enterprises. In 2010 it generated €19.2 billion of value added, representing 3% of the manufacturing total (DG Enterprise and Industry, 2013). Italy and the new EU member states (i.e. Romania, Poland, and Bulgaria) are the largest employers, while Italy, France, Germany, Spain, and the UK lead the sector in terms of added value.

The wearing apparel sector is a mature sector characterised by a rather low capacity for technological innovation and high competitive pressure (European Commission, 2006; Taplin, 2006). This is a result, among others, of a very high labour intensity of the sector which leaves very little room for technological, capital-intensive innovations. For example, sewing techniques remained almost unchanged during the last century (Nordas, 2004; OECD, 2004). Similarly the OECD classified the sector as a low-technology industry (OECD 2011). Hence, redesigning business models towards more sustainability may offer companies in the sector a unique opportunity to differentiate themselves from their competitors (Schmitt and Renken, 2012). However, social and environmental challenges are varied and spread throughout the supply chain. Companies, therefore, have to ask themselves where the largest potentials for improvement lie and in which areas such improvements may be translated into new business models and genuine competitive advantage (Martinuzzi and Krumay, 2013).

Our paper provides an overview of the most critical social and environmental effects of the sector, as perceived by a set of sectoral experts, and the extent to which they are currently tackled by CSR initiatives in companies. On this basis, our paper offers a future-oriented perspective on CSR in the wearing apparel sector. We explore the future importance of CSR in the context of important sectoral trends. Our analysis may help to identify the areas where better managing social and environmental issues creates a large potential for differentiation from competitors, and thus may inspire the emergence of sustainable business models in the wearing apparel sector.

Contextual contingencies, CSR, and sustainable business models

Currently, the wearing apparel sector is relatively under-investigated in terms of sustainable business models. At the same time, the sector causes significant social and environmental effects related to its operations, manufacturing processes, and its global supply chains. Indeed, many environmental and social effects attributable to the European wearing apparel sector materialise in developing countries. In the area of environmental effects of the sector, concerns are mainly related to resource use and waste generation (Gwilt and Rissanen, 2011; Draper et al., 2007). In the social realm, issues are related to the quality of jobs in those countries where the mainstay of manufacturing takes place, including labour conditions and human rights issues (Gereffi and Memedovic, 2003).

In this paper, we investigate if and to what extent quality of jobs and environmental issues may inspire the development of sustainable business models in the wearing apparel sector now and in the future. By doing so we do not aim at developing any specific business model but rather attempt to recognise and highlight these contingencies, which we posit to be pertinent for the design of new business models. We attempt to we meet this goal by answering the following research questions:

▶ Which are the most relevant environmental and quality of jobs issues affected by the wearing apparel sector? How is their importance expected to develop in the future?

▶ How are individual environmental and quality of jobs issues currently being impacted by CSR? How is the level of CSR with regard to these issues expected to develop in the future?

▶ What are the most important sectoral trends expected to be influential in the future? What effects are they likely to have on CSR?

In its analytical approach, our paper links up to two mature debates in the areas of management and corporate social responsibility (CSR), namely the contingency approach (Rumelt, 1974; Mintzberg, 1979) and the discussion around the business case for CSR (Carroll and Shabana, 2010; Margolis and Walsh, 2003). The former helps explain why external social and environmental issues may pressure companies in the highly competitive environment of the wearing apparel industry to move towards more sustainable business models. In combination with the latter discussion, sustainability challenges in the industry may be framed as a field of opportunity and growth that companies may use to gain competitive advantage (see also Schmitt and Renken, 2012; Moore *et al.*, 2012). There is thus a reactive (i.e. responding to external pressure), a proactive (i.e. recognising business opportunities), and even an anticipatory (i.e. responding to future trends) dimension to the debate around sustainable business models in the wearing apparel industry.

The basic proposition of the contingency approach holds that external contingency factors influence the way companies design their strategies and business models. This includes social and environmental issues and expectations towards them. Hart and Milstein (1999, 2003) argue that such concerns and expectations have significant implications for companies, their business models, and the creation of a shareholder value. In the area of sustainability and CSR research, Husted (2000) used the approach to show that corporate social performance is a function of the fit between the nature of a given social issue, and the strategies and structures that companies introduce to address it. This view was further discussed (Keijzers, 2002; Borland, 2009; Hall *et al.*, 2010) and taken up by several studies investigating the influence of corporate sustainability on corporate performance (Lopez *et al.*, 2007; Hockerts and Wustenhagen, 2010; Surroca *et al.*, 2010). Carroll and Shabana (2010) reviewed the business case for CSR and argued that the relationship between CSR and financial performance depends on situational contingencies and differs from company to company.

We argue in this paper that sustainable business models may create competitive advantage in those cases where companies anticipate or proactively engage with a social or environmental issue, thus realising a first mover advantage and acting as rule makers for the whole sector. Indeed, the way companies innovate their business models may well determine their organisational survival and resilience to ever tighter competition (de Oliveira Teixeira and Werther, 2013). Given that external contingencies seem to play out differently depending on the situational context (Carroll and Shabana, 2010), it is useful to limit the analysis to one economic sector in order to ensure a basic level of homogeneity among the companies addressed. While several practitioner guidelines on CSR already offer sector-specific supplements (e.g. the Global Reporting Initiative's Sector Supplements), only very few studies have so far dealt with sector specificities of CSR. As one of very few authors to date, Maccarone (2009) posits that a deeper understanding of sector-specific elements of CSR is a prerequisite for explaining emerging analogies and differences between sectors. This view is confirmed by Martinuzzi (2011) who investigated sector-specific linkages between CSR and competitiveness.

The wearing apparel industry represents an interesting case for such a sector-specific investigation, as it is a mature industry with rather low capacity for technological innovation and high competitive pressure. Thus, redesigning business models towards sustainability may offer the industry a unique opportunity if companies manage to identify the 'right' contingencies. This would entail developing sustainable business models that create a double dividend, in terms of tackling an environmental or social issue of concern while also gaining competitive advantage (Schmitt and Renken, 2012; Martinuzzi and Krumay, 2013).

The term 'business models' has become widely applied in practice and research, although a universally accepted definition of the concept is not yet at hand. According to Teece (2010) 'A business model articulates the logic, the data, and other evidence that support a value proposition for the customer and a viable structure of revenues and costs for the enterprise delivering that value'. Over the last decade, novel business models, which also integrate social aspects, have started to be widely discussed, especially in a development context. This includes social entrepreneurship approaches, bottom-of-pyramid models or micro-credit schemes. The drive towards more CSR as regards the environmental effects from business operations goes back even further. For instance, Levi Strauss, a global producer of jeans, has launched several sustainability initiatives such as Water<Less, which aims at using less water in the finishing process. Another example is Puma's InCycle project designing and offering biodegradable or recyclable products (Rahbek-Nielsen et al., 2013).

However, the current understanding of sustainable business models and their operationalisation on the corporate level is still weak (Stubbs and Cocklin, 2008). One of very few attempts at getting to the bottom of how businesses transition to sustainable business models was made by Benn et al. (2006) who developed an integrated phase model for understanding how companies shift towards social and ecological sustainability. One important conclusion from their research and other scholars' work is that truly sustainable business models depend on the integration of CSR at the strategic level (see also Lantos, 2001; Husted and Allen, 2007; Siegel and Vitaliano, 2007; Heslin and Ochoa, 2008; Porter and Kramer, 2011).

Sector effects on the environment and quality of jobs

The importance of business for furthering global economic and social development is well established. Corporations invest in foreign countries, provide jobs, and thus generate formalised labour relations and income. They promote education and training, and make products and services available. They buy products and services themselves (B2B), thus furthering specialised suppliers. Finally, they pay taxes that contribute to the provision of public services (de Mello, 1999; Moran, 1998). At the same time, corporate conduct is receiving substantial criticism. Among other things, business is accused of supporting exploitative employment conditions and human rights abuses (e.g. Jonassen,

2008; Kinley and Joseph, 2002), causing environmental deterioration (e.g. Adeola, 2001), furthering corruption (e.g. Mauro, 1995, 1997), and failing to mainstream responsible conduct in developing countries (see Blowfield, 2012).

The wearing apparel industry has become an important component in this equation due to its reliance on global supply chains in the wake of the large-scale relocation of manufacturing and raw material supply to developing countries. As many links of the upstream value chain have been relocated, so have many of the environmental and quality of jobs issues attributed to the industry. Today, the industry is perceived as being responsible for many negative effects on the environment and quality of jobs issues. The sector is being continuously criticised for perpetuating unfavourable labour conditions, not only within developing countries (Nordas, 2004; OECD, 2004). These are frequently aggravated by weak domestic institutional and economic framework conditions in developing and transition countries. The sector is also accused of slave-like conditions (Kaufman, 2006), child labour (Emmelhainz and Adams, 1999; Overeem and Peepercamp, 2012), mistreatment of women (Kaufman et al., 2004; Welford and Frost, 2006), and violating human rights (Emmelhainz and Adams, 1999; Dickson and Eckman, 2006). For instance, Barendt and Musiolek (2005) interviewed 256 workers from 55 workplaces in Eastern Europe and Turkey. He found that they were paid below living wages and were forced to take on additional jobs, mainly in agriculture. Goos and Manning (2007) and the Low Pay Commission (2010) confirmed that jobs in the textile industry are among the least paid occupations in the UK, with a high share of workers being paid below the national minimum salary. Barendt and Musiolek (2005), Michalski and Grobelny (2007) and Madsen et al. (2007) report that health and working standards are frequently violated, especially in terms of work load, exposure to hazardous substances, body posture and movement.

Regarding environmental effects of the sector, its energy, water and chemicals intensity are among the primary concerns. Environmental effects start at the farm level, when toxic chemicals are used to support growth of cotton (insecticides, fungicides). In the case of synthetics (which represent more than 60% of fibre production), the most important resource is oil, hence production of synthetic fibres leads to exploitation of fossil fuels: directly, because of production processes, as well as indirectly, because of processes involved in extracting and refining the oil (Müller-Christ and Gandenberg, 2006). Regardless of the type of fabrics and their final destination, most of them go through wet processing, which consists of cleaning, bleaching, dyeing, and finishing in an aqueous environment. Wet processing puts enormous pressure on the environment, as it requires great amounts of water and large volumes of toxic substances (Kirian-Ciliz, 2003). The industry is also responsible for high waste volumes resulting from 'fast fashion' (Allwood et al., 2006), which is a business model focused on capturing current high fashion trends, quick design and manufacturing at a low-end market price.

In light of increasing societal pressures on companies in the wearing apparel industry to tackle these issues, its role in furthering sustainable development has been increasingly raised in recent years (Dobers and Halme, 2009;

Blowfield, 2012). The development of more sustainable business models in the highly globalised wearing apparel industry is thus increasingly being driven by processes at the global level as well and presents a chance for companies in the sector to manage reputational risk and seize new business opportunities.

Methodological approach

In order to answer the research questions presented in the previous sections we used data collected in the course of two European research projects: 'Responsible Competitiveness' and 'IMPACT'. In the 'Responsible Competitiveness' project (funded by DG Enterprise, see Martinuzzi *et al.*, 2011) we explored the impacts of CSR on competitiveness, assessed a transnational sectoral initiative within the wearing apparel sector and carried out ten qualitative in-depth interviews with sectoral experts from research, from business associations and from trade unions. For the analyses we applied methods of qualitative content analysis (Krippendorf, 1980; Titscher *et al.*, 1998; Mayring, 2000) and identified substantive statements (Gilham, 2000). The interview transcripts were subjected to an inductive coding process with a view to eliciting recurring themes and statements on: 1) important environmental issues in the sector as perceived by the interviewees; and 2) important issues regarding the quality of jobs in the sector as perceived by the interviewees. The coded content units were subsequently fed into environmental and quality of jobs issue categories. The preliminary categories developed through content analysis were triangulated against a comprehensive analysis of recent sectoral trends (see Martinuzzi *et al.*, 2011) and subsequently revised.

In the course of the whole IMPACT project and the Europe wide survey, we defined CSR as 'actions that appear to further some social good, beyond the interest of the firm and that which is required by law' (McWilliams and Siegel, 2001:117). Although there is no widely accepted definition of CSR the one by McWilliams and Siegel (2001) seemed to receive a reasonable support among scholars and stressed the voluntary and beyond compliance nature of activities labelled as CSR.

Based on the categories developed through the content analysis, we carried out a large online-expert-survey in summer 2012 in the course of the FP7-project 'IMPACT' (www.csr-impact.eu). The sector in focus was wearing apparel, which is a subsector of the textile industry according to the NACE 2.0 classification of economic activities (Eurostat, 2008). Through the implementation of the survey, we significantly broadened our outreach by addressing a much higher number of experts from all across Europe, by explicitly including corporate experts in our panel and by ensuring that the number and composition of experts mirrors the relative importance of the wearing apparel sector in the different European countries. In accordance with the research questions and based on the previously developed categorisation of issue areas, the questionnaire consisted of parts, which can be classified as follows:

1. Sectoral effects on the natural environment and quality of jobs issues

2. Impacts of CSR on the identified sectoral effects

3. Expected future importance of CSR

4. Expected future trends in the sector and their influence on the role of CSR

In selecting the experts we targeted respondents from different institutional backgrounds and of balanced geographical spread. Selection of experts was not random, but motivated by willingness to achieve a sample of respondents representing a wide variety of organisational affiliations and opinions towards CSR. The stratified sample consisted of three types of strata: business experts, scholars and stakeholders. The survey covered all EU member countries, with the addition of Switzerland, Turkey and Norway. Overall, we invited 255 experts from the wearing apparel sector. Almost half of them were CSR managers, sustainability managers or general managers from companies, which were identified using the AMADEUS database.[1] The second part of the sample consisted of scholars and stakeholders from business associations, NGOs, universities,[2] research centres, and public authorities. All of the experts were selected according to their expertise concerning environmental and quality of jobs issues, CSR in the wearing apparel sector, and overall sector expertise. Our survey was online from June to August 2012. Overall, 79 experts participated in our survey, resulting in a response rate of about 31%.[3] The final sample exhibited a relatively comprehensive view on CSR in the wearing apparel sector:

▶ **Expert groups.** 53% of the respondents are scholars, 33% represent the business sector (corporate managers or consultants) and 14% stakeholders (such as NGOs and labour unions). Therefore a well-balanced view of different interest groups can be guaranteed

▶ **Region.** The respondents represent Central Europe (35%), the Mediterranean (22%) countries, the Anglo-Saxon regions (15%), Scandinavia (11%), the new EU member states (8%) and the non-EU countries of Europe (9%). Therefore our study covers the economic structure of Europe in an appropriate way

▶ **Level.** 47% of the experts who participated in our study work at top management level, 34% middle management and 10% are non-management

---

1 Database of comparable financial and business information on Europe's biggest 520,000 public and private companies by assets (www.amadeus.bvdinfo.com).

2 Scholars of the wearing apparel sector (and broader textile industry) were selected based on their sector-specific publications retrieved through journal database SCOPUS.

3 Although there is no commonly accepted standard for the online survey response rate, some studies suggest that the response achieved in this study is considerable and sufficient. According to Hamilton (2009), who reviewed 199 online surveys, the average response rate of online surveys is 32.52%. Another review of 31 studies from 1995 to 2000 by Sheehan (2001) showed an average response rate of 36.83%.

professionals. Their high level of expertise ensures that our findings represent the best available knowledge on the wearing apparel sector

In accordance with the first research question, we asked experts to assess the effects of the wearing apparel sector on certain environmental and quality of job issues. In addition they were asked to predict how these effects are likely to develop during the next five years. Dealing with the second research question, we asked the experts to assess the influence of CSR on these issues and, again, about their future development. Environmental and quality of jobs issues as well as the influence of CSR on them were measured on a Likert-scale from 1 (low) to 5 (high), while possible answers for their future development were: decrease, stay the same, and increase. Addressing the third research question, the experts were asked to assess the future importance of CSR, as well as likeliness of certain sectoral trends and their influence on CSR. Both questions were measured using a Likert-scale from 1 (low) to 5 (high). The use of Likert scales is a standard and widely established way of measuring attitudes and perceptions, generating ordinal data (Likert, 1932; Allen and Seaman, 2007). In our survey they enabled the consistent and standardised questioning of respondents in accordance with our categorisation of environmental and quality of jobs issues.

In analysing the data we carried out non-parametric, descriptive analyses for each question which are presented in the next section of this paper. In order to control for biases and identify any potential differences in the responses from different groups of experts or between experts representing different European regions, we conducted a Mann-Whitney U-test, which is a non-parametric test verifying a null hypothesis that two populations are the same, against an alternative hypothesis that one of the two populations has higher values than the other one (Mann and Whitney, 1947). While a certain self-selection bias cannot be avoided in online surveys, the Mann-Whitney U-test helped us establish that neither the organisational affiliation nor the regional affiliation of respondents explained the variation in results. We found no significant differences between the responses of different groups. In the following, the findings of our analysis are laid out in detail.

Findings

The most influential set of development goals to date are the Millennium Development Goals (MDGs). Along with the ILO core conventions, they may provide orientation for companies in the wearing apparel sector wishing to engage in more CSR throughout their supply chains. While the main responsibility for achieving the MDGs lies with governments, they affect the socio-economic context of a globalised economy in which companies operate. European experts on the wearing apparel sector see the largest potential impacts of CSR for achieving global development goals in three specific areas: ensuring environmental sustainability, eradicating child labour, and improving health, safety, and working conditions (see Figure 1).

Figure 1 Potential contribution of CSR in the wearing apparel sector to achieving global development goals

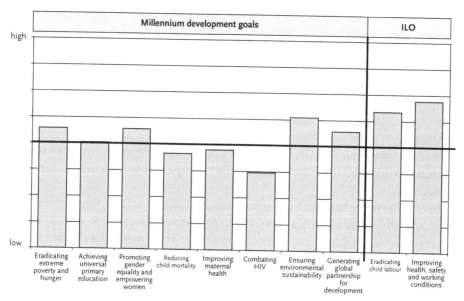

While global effects of the wearing apparel sector are difficult to measure since they are frequently indirect and localised, it is notable that there seems to be a general tendency among sector experts to recognise the positive effects that CSR is already having in development countries. Labour related concerns covered by the ILO conventions seem to be more successfully tackled at present than the more remote general development goals reflected in the MDGs. This confirms the relevance of the emphasis this paper is placing on quality of jobs issues. Among the MDGs, 'Ensuring environmental sustainability' emerged as the most relevant development goal, coinciding with our focus on environmental effects of the wearing apparel sector.

This is a first indication that sustainable business models addressing those global development issues might hold a potential for building on existing efforts in the area of CSR. In the following, we present a more precise analysis of the environmental and quality of jobs issues that might also provide interesting angles for companies to gain competitive advantage.

Environmental issues in the wearing apparel sector

Survey participants were asked to rate the relative importance of the sector's effects on environmental issues divided into the following categories: CO_2 & energy, hazardous substances, raw materials & waste, water, and other supply chain effects (e.g. use of water during cotton cultivation). The result was a comprehensive rating, which reflects the environmental issues that experts from the sector are familiar with and aware of. In addition, the rating allows some insight into which key effects are perceived as relatively more relevant. According to the respondents, the most significant environmental issues in the wearing apparel sector are environmental effects in the supply chain, use of raw materials and waste generation, and use of water from both plant cultivation and manufacturing (see Figure 2).

Respondents were then asked to indicate their expectation on how the relevance of the identified environmental effects would develop in the future. For each effect the experts indicated whether they expected its relative importance to increase, to decrease, or to remain the same over the next five years. The findings show that some environmental effects are expected to increase in relevance in the future, most importantly the use of raw materials and waste generation as well as supply chain effects. The relevance of hazardous substances use in manufacturing and toxic waste generation is expected to remain the same or to decrease.

In order to relate the identified environmental effects to CSR, the experts were subsequently asked to indicate to what degree these effects were already being successfully tackled by companies in the sector. This involved a similar rating exercise, this time concerning the relative effects of CSR. The rating exercise revealed that CSR is perceived as most impactful when directed at hazardous substances, use of energy in textile manufacturing and water use in manufacturing. Respondents expected the effects of CSR to increase across the board in

Figure 2 Current and future environmental effects of the sector and impacts of CSR on them

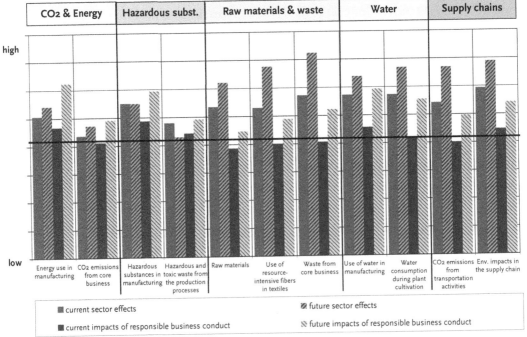

the future, indicating that CSR will become significantly more important over the coming five years. The increase was especially pronounced in the areas of waste generation, water consumption and energy use.

The ratings were then contrasted with each other to reveal the 'CSR gap' between those environmental effects rated as most relevant and current levels of CSR. Interestingly, the survey showed that hazardous substances in manufacturing, and use of energy and CO_2 emissions from textile manufacturing were relatively well tackled by CSR activities, but not perceived as the most relevant environmental effects in the wearing apparel sector. This was reflected in the rather small gap between the assessment of these concerns and effects of CSR on them. In other cases, however, such as use of raw materials and environmental effects in the supply chain, use of water and waste from fast fashion, which belong to the top-rated environmental sector effects, a large gap was identified. This finding shows that current efforts in CSR are not perceived as tackling these issues effectively. The same holds for the future: our findings indicate that the expected increase in CSR will not be enough to compensate for the expected growth of negative effects in the key areas of supply chains and raw materials and waste. Indeed, the gaps between the expected future importance of key supply chain effects and effects related to raw materials and waste generation are expected to widen considerably in the future.

Quality of jobs issues in the wearing apparel sector

In order to identify the most relevant quality of jobs effects of the wearing apparel sector, rating exercises were carried out with the respondents, congruent with those used to identify the most relevant environmental issues. The experts were asked to rate the relative importance of the sector's effects on two key issue areas: human rights and equality and job quality.

Experts rated sector effects on human rights, safety, health and working conditions as well as wages as being of the highest concern for the sector. For each issue the experts then indicated whether they expected its relative importance to increase, to decrease or to remain the same over the next five years. The findings show that effects of the sector on all quality of jobs effects are expected to increase in importance in the future. This trend is particularly visible in regards to safety, health and working conditions, human rights and job security.

In order to relate the identified quality of jobs effects to CSR, the experts were subsequently asked to indicate in how far these effects were already being successfully tackled by companies in the sector. This involved a similar rating exercise, this time concerning the relative effects of CSR activities. When asked to rate the perceived effects of CSR on quality of jobs issues, the respondents gave the highest ratings to corporate efforts on human rights, safety, health and working conditions, and diversity (see Figure 3). For all quality of jobs issues the respondents expect an increase in CSR efforts to tackle them more effectively in the future. This trend is most pronounced for human rights, safety, health and working conditions, diversity and job security.

Figure 3 Current and future quality of jobs concerns in the sector and impacts of
CSR on them

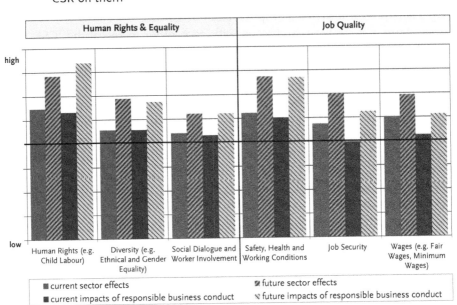

As for environmental issues, the ratings on quality of jobs effects and current
CSR effects were then contrasted with each other. The survey did not show many
substantial gaps between quality of jobs effects and effects of CSR on them.
In most cases CSR seems to be relatively well matched to the level of negative
quality of jobs effects. This indicates that these issues are already at the forefront
of corporate efforts to act responsibly. Noticeable gaps between sectoral effects
and CSR effects concerned job security and wages.

Emerging trends in and the future importance of CSR

In accordance with the contingency approach, environmental and quality of
jobs issues may be translated into an impetus for CSR and, ultimately, the
emergence of more sustainable business models. However, the pathway of this
transition is a complex one. Indeed it is beyond the scope of this paper to establish a comprehensive causal chain from contingency to sustainable business
model. However, it is important to recall that the extent to which contingencies
are translated into more CSR are situational and sector-specific (Carroll and
Shabana, 2010), i.e. dependent on future trends specific to the wearing apparel
sector.

The survey findings suggest that CSR will be of growing importance in the
near future. More than 61% of the respondents answered that they expect the
role of CSR to become more prominent in the sector during the next five years,
while only 8% foresaw a decline. Notwithstanding this positive outlook, the
respondents also clearly indicated that the efforts expended by companies on
CSR might well hinge on a number of (macro-) economic and political trends,
the rate of innovation within the sector, as well as societal trends (see Figure 4).

In addition we conducted a Mann-Whitney U-test in order to verify if the perceived future role of CSR varies in the eyes of respondents coming from different fields; i.e. from businesses, trade associations, academia, critical NGOs and trade unions. These experts' opinions may vary substantially e.g. trade unionists and NGOs tend to be very critical about CSR activities as they are often perceived as a means to relax or postpone new regulations. However, the performed test revealed no significant differences between respondents' opinions, which proves coherence of their answers concerning the future role of CSR.

Respondents expected externally driven trends in the general economy, policy and society at large to have a larger influence on future levels of CSR than the internal rate of innovation. Most prominently, the sector experts expect growing competitive pressure and more stringent (EU) regulations to impose new constraints on companies in the wearing apparel sector. These trends are expected to be translated into more CSR at the company level. Equally, rising consumer demand for fair working conditions in fashion and the increasing role of labels are expected to incentivise more CSR from the bottom up. These findings indicate that the previously identified and reported environmental and quality of jobs contingencies might well be funnelled through growing economic and political pressures and societal expectations towards companies to act responsibly.

Figure 4 Future trends in the sector and their influence on the role of CSR

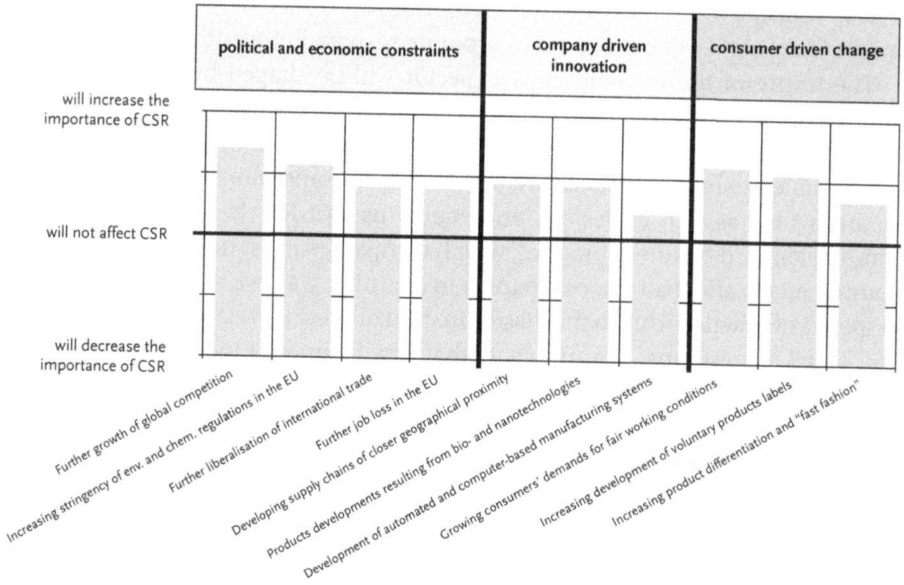

Discussion and concluding remarks

Our study sheds light on the contingency factors which might hold potential for developing sustainable business models in the wearing apparel sector. Based on a Europe-wide expert survey, we identified the current and future environmental and quality of jobs issues, which are perceived as the most relevant in the wearing apparel sector. In addition, we examined the effects of corporate responsible behaviour on these concerns and highlighted some gaps between the identified environmental issues and the effects of CSR on them. Finally, we investigated the future importance of CSR (and future trends stimulating such conduct), which might lead to development of the sustainable business models. Our findings lead us to several conclusions, which might be weighed heavily from the companies' perspective.

Corporate responsible conduct is not a management fashion—this is true in general, and particularly for the wearing apparel sector, as our study showed. Explicitly asked about the future of CSR, 61% of our respondents expected an increase in the importance of responsible business practices and only 8% anticipated a decrease. This general impression was also mirrored in their expectations concerning the future developments of CSR effects on the identified environmental and quality of job issues. In only 1 issue area out of 17, the sectoral effects are expected to decrease, while all other sectoral effects as well as the effects of CSR on them will increase—some of them substantially. Respondents' assessment of the sector-specific trends revealed the same tendency: regardless of whether these trends are caused by political or economic constraints, by innovation or by a change of consumer preferences, all of them are expected to increase the importance of CSR. This leads us to the conclusion that all innovative business models—regardless of which particular aspect they might focus on—will have to take corporate responsibility into account.

The future of the wearing apparel sector will be shaped by several contingencies related to the environment and quality of job issues. Many of them are expected to become more important in the future while the contributions of responsible business practices are expected to become more powerful as well. In areas such as CO_2 emissions and energy use, CSR is becoming more and more a standard business practice, which companies must not ignore. As these contingencies affect all the companies in a similar way, we expect certain convergence of practices due to the dissemination of product-related, technological, and social innovations. We anticipate that new business models in these areas will rather witness certain incremental diversifications within the limitations of the contingencies we found, but not radical new solutions.

We argue that the study findings bring certain insights for companies willing to differentiate themselves from competitors along the social and environmental lines. Our study showed that some environmental and quality of jobs concerns will become much more important in the future, while the expected solutions resulting from CSR are comparably low. These gaps are potential points of intervention where innovative business models can bring to the fore a double dividend of competitive advantage and significant contributions to sustainability. These gaps can be found in regards to the use of raw materials, waste creation as well as job security and wages. This opens up a potential for differentiation through organisational and business practices, which is highly valued by certain consumers.

Developing innovative business models in these areas will allow companies to become pioneers, rule-breakers and even rule-makers (Martinuzzi and Krumay, 2013).[4] While our study aimed at identifying future macro-trends and contingencies and thus can serve as an important source of information for the development of new business models, future research will need to assess their operationalisation and success factors on a micro-level. In order to gain insights into the development and implementation of such business models we would encourage accompanying research and case studies.

References

Adeola, F. (2001) 'Environmental Injustice and Human Rights Abuse: The States, MNCs, and Repression of Minority Groups in the World System', In: Human Ecology Review 8, 1, S. 39–59, http://www.nigerianlawguru.com/articles/environmental%20law/ENVI RONMENTAL%20INJUSTICE%20AND%20HUMAN%20RIGHTS%20ABUSE.pdf.

Allen, I. E., Seaman, C. A. (2007) 'Likert scales and data analyses', Quality Progress, 40, 7, 64-65.

Allwood, J.M., Laursen, S.F., Malvido de Rodriguez, C., Bocken, N.M.P. (2006) 'Well dressed? The present and future sustainability of clothing and textiles in the United Kingdom', University of Cambridge Institute for Manufacturing, Cambridge, UK, www .ifm.eng.cam.ac.uk/sustainability/projects/mass/UK_textiles.pdf.

Anderson, C.R., Zeithaml, C.P. (1984) 'Stage of the product life cycle, business strategy, and business performance', Academy of Management Journal, 27, 1, 5-24.

Barendt, R., Musiolek, B. (2005), 'Workers' voices. The situation of women in Eastern European and Turkish garment industries', Clean Clothes Campaign, Evangelische Akademie Meißen.

Benn, S., Dunphy, D., Griffiths, A. (2006) 'Enabling change for corporate sustainability: An integrated perspective', Australasian Journal of Environmental Management, 13, 156-165.

Blowfield, M. (2012) 'Business and development: making sense of business as a development agent', Corporate Governance, 12, 4, 414-426.

Borland, H. (2009) 'Conceptualising global strategic sustainability and corporate transformational change', International Marketing Review, 26, 4/5, 554-572.

Bourne M., Kennerley M., Franco-Santos M. (2005) 'Managing through measures: a study of impact on performance', Journal of Manufacturing Technology Management, 16, 4, 373-395.

Campbell, L. (2007) 'Why would corporations behave in socially responsible ways? An institutional theory of corporate social responsibility', Academy of Management Review, 32, 3, 946-67.

Carroll, A. B., Shabana K.M. (2010) 'The business case for corporate social responsibility: a review of concepts, research and practice', International Journal of Management Reviews, 12, 1, 85-105.

---

4 Cp., for instance, Morgan's (2015, in this issue) study on Marks & Spencer's gradual integration of sustainability innovation into its business model and Hvass' (2015, in this issue) take on end-of life product innovation.

Chi, T., Kilduff, P. (2010) 'An empirical investigation of the determinants and shifting patterns of US apparel imports using a gravity model framework', Journal of Fashion Marketing & Management, 14, 3, 501-520.

Christensen, H.K., Montgomery, C. (1981) 'Corporate economic performance: Diversification strategy versus market structure', Strategic Management Journal, 2, 327-343.

De Oliveira Teixeira, P., Werther, W.B. (2013) 'Resilience: Continuous renewal of competitive advantages', Business Horizons, 56, 3, 333-342.

DG Enterprise and Industry (2013), http://ec.europa.eu/enterprise/sectors/textiles/index_en.htm.

Dickson, M. A., Eckman M. (2006) 'Social Responsibility: The Concept As Defined by Apparel and Textile Scholars', Clothing and Textiles Research Journal, 24, 3, 178-91.

Dickson, M. A., Waters, Y., & López-Gydosh, D. (2012). Stakeholder Expectations for Environmental Performance within the Apparel Industry. Journal of Corporate Citizenship, (45).

Dobers, P., Halme, M. (2009) 'Corporate social responsibility and developing countries', Corporate Social Responsibility and Environmental Management, 16, 5, 237-249.

Doucouliagos, H., Paldam, M. (2009) 'The aid effectiveness literature: The sad results of 40 years of research', Journal of Economic Surveys, 23, 433–61.

Draper, S., Murray, V., & Weissbrod, I. (2007). Fashioning sustainability: A review of sustainability impacts of the clothing industry. In Forum for the Future (pp. 1-14).

Emmelhainz, M.A., Adams, R. J. (1999) 'The Apparel Industry Response to "Sweatshop" Concerns: A Review and Analysis of Codes of Conduct', The Journal of Supply Chain Management, 35, 3, 51-57.

EURATEX (2009) 'The EU27 Textile and Clothing industry in the year 2008', Adinolfi, R. in EURATEX General Assembly 5/62009, http://www.euratex.org/content/the-eu-27-textile-and-clothing-industry-year-2008.

European Commission (2006) European textiles and Clothing in a quota free environment: 2nd Report of the High Level Group, http://ec.europa.eu/enterprise/sectors/textiles/files/hlg_report_18_09_06_en.pdf

European Commission (2009) 'European industry in a changing word. Updated sectoral overview 2009'.

Eurostat (2008) NACE 2.0 Statistical classification of economic activities in the European Community, http://epp.eurostat.ec.europa.eu/cache/ITY_OFFPUB/KS-RA-07-015/EN/KS-RA-07-015-EN.PDF.

Eurostat (2009) 'European Business: Facts and figures', http://epp.eurostat.ec.europa.eu/cache/ITY_OFFPUB/KS-CD-09-001/EN/KS-CD-09-001-EN.PDF.

Flynn, B.B., Huo, B., Zhao, X. (2010) 'The impact of supply chain integration on performance: A contingency and configuration approach', Journal of Operations Management, 28, 1, 58-71.

Fox, T., Ward, H., Howard, B. (2002) 'Public sector roles in strengthening corporate social responsibility: A baseline study', The World Bank, Washington, DC.

Friedman, A. L., Miles S. (2001) 'Socially responsible investment and corporate social and environmental reporting in the UK: an exploratory study', The British Accounting Review, 33, 4, 523-48.

Gereffi, G., & Memedovic, O. (2003) The global apparel value chain: What prospects for upgrading by developing countries (pp. 3-11). Vienna: United Nations Industrial Development Organization.

Gillham, B. (2000) Case study research methods. London, Continuum.

Goos, M., Manning, A. (2007) 'Lousy and lovely jobs: The rising polarization of work in Britain', The Review of Economics and Statistics, 89, 1, 118-33.

Gordon, L.A., Loeb, M.P., Tseng, C-Y. (2009), 'Enterprise risk management and firm performance: A contingency perspective', Journal of Accounting and Public Policy, 28, 4, 301-327.

Greenhill, R., Prizzon, A. (2012) 'The Aid Effectiveness Agenda: The benefits of going ahead', EDCSP.

Groves, R. M., Fowler Jr, F. J., Couper, M. P., Lepkowski, J. M., Singer, E. and Tourangeau, R. (2009) Survey methodology, Wiley.

Gwilt, A., & Rissanen, T. (Eds.) (2011) Shaping sustainable fashion: changing the way we make and use clothes. Routledge.

Hall, J., Daneke, G., Lenox, M. (2010) 'Sustainable development and entrepreneurship: Past contributions and future directions', Journal of Business Venturing, 25, 5, 439-448.

Hambrick, D.C. (1983) 'High profit strategies in mature capital goods industries: A contingency approach', Academy of Management Journal, 26, 687-707.

Hamilton, M. B. (2003). Online survey response rates and times: Background and guidance for industry. Tercent, Inc. Retrieved February, 4, 2009.

Harrigan, K. (1980) 'Strategy Formulation in Declining Industries', Academy of Management Review, 5, 4, 599-604.

Harrigan, K.R. (1982) 'Exit decisions in mature industries', Academy of Management Journal, 25, 707-732.

Hart S.L., Milstein M.B. (2003) 'Creating sustainable value', Academy of Management Executive, 17, 2, 56-69.

Hart, S.L., Milstein, M.B. (1999) 'Global sustainability and the creative destruction of industries', Sloan Management Review, 41, 1, 23-33.

Hatten, K.J., Schnedel D.E. (1977) 'Heterogenity within an industry: Firm conduct in the brewing industry', Journal of Industrial Economics, 26, 97-113.

Heslin, P. A., Ochoa J. D. (2008) 'Understanding and developing strategic corporate social responsibility', Organizational Dynamics, 37, 2, 125-44.

Hockerts, K., Wüstenhagen, R. (2010) 'Greening Goliaths versus emerging Davids: Theorizing about the role of incumbents and new entrants in sustainable entrepreneurship', Journal of Business Venturing, 25, 5, 481-492.

Hofer, C. W. (1975) 'Toward a contingency theory of business strategy', Academy of Management Journal, 18, 784–810.

Husted, B. W., Allen, D.B. (2007) 'Strategic Corporate Social Responsibility and Value Creation among Large Firms: Lessons from the Spanish Experience', Long Range Planning, 40, 6, 594-610.

Husted, B.W. (2000) 'Toward a model of cross-cultural business ethics: the impact of individualism and collectivism on the ethical decision-making process', Academy of Management Proceedings & Membership Directory, I1-I6.

ILO (2013) www.ilo.org/global/about-the-ilo/activities/all/WCMS_218693/lang--en/index.htm.

Jackson, G., Apostolakou, A. (2010) 'Corporate Social Responsibility in Western Europe: An Institutional Mirror or Substitute?' Journal of Business Ethics, 94, 3, 371-394.

Jonassen, F. (2008) 'A Baby-Step to Global Labor Reform: Corporate Codes of Conduct and the Child', Barry University School of Law, http://lawweb3.law.umn.edu/uploads/8A/te/8Ate-ibGnirgrwFTcA-Jrw/Jonassen-Final-Online-PDF-04.07.09.pdf, zuletzt aktualisiert am 07.04.2009, Last accessed 08.01.2013.

Jones, R.M., Hayes, S.G. (2004) 'The UK clothing industry. Extinction or evolution?', Journal of Fashion Marketing and Management, 8, 3, 262-78.

Kaufman, A., Tiantubtim, E., Pussayabipul, N. (2004) 'Implementing voluntary labour standards and codes of conduct in the Thai garment industry', The Journal of Corporate Citizenship, 13, 91-9.

Kaufman, J.V. (2006) 'Principles of Contemporary Corporate Governance', Australian Business Law Review, 34, 3, 246.

Keijzers, G. (2002) 'The transition to the sustainable enterprise', Journal of Cleaner Production, 10, 4, 349.

Kharas, H. (2010) 'Can aid catalyze development?' In: Making development aid more effective. Washington, DC: The Brookings Institute, 3-9.

Ki-Hoon, L. (2009) 'Why and how to adopt green management into business organizations?', Management Decision, 47, 7, 1101-1121.

Kinley, D., Joseph, S. (2002) 'Multinational corporations and human rights. Questions about their relationship', In: Alternative LJ 27 (1), S., 7–11, http://christchurchdarfur.org/pdf/global_business/darfur_-_04_Dec_-_Castan_Centre.pdf.

Kirian-Ciliz, N. (2003) 'Reduction in resources consumption by process modifications in cotton wet processes', Journal of Cleaner Production, 11, 481-86.

Krippendorff, K. (1980) Content analysis. An Introduction to its Methodology. Beverly Hills: Sage.

Lantos, G. P. (2001) 'The boundaries of strategic corporate social responsibility', Journal of Consumer Marketing, 18, 7, 595-632.

Likert, R. (1932) 'A technique for the measurement of attitudes', Archives of Psychology.

López-Pérez, M., Perez-Lopez, M., Rodriguez-Ariza, L. (2007) 'The Opinions of European Companies on Corporate Social Responsibility and Its Relation to Innovation', Issues in Social & Environmental Accounting, 1, 2, 276-295.

Maccarone, E.M. (2002) 'Making Social Science Matter (Book)', Social Science Journal, 39, 1, 146.

Maccarrone, P. (2009) Factors influencing the attitude towards corporate social responsibility: Some empirical evidence from Italy. Corporate Governance, Vol. 9(2), pp. 103-119.

Madsen, J., Hartlin, B., Perumalpillai, S., Selby, S., Aumonier, S. (2007) 'Mapping of evidence on sustainable development impacts that occur in life cycles of clothing: A report to the Department for Environment, Food and Rural Affairs', Environmental Resources Management Ltd Defra, London, randd.defra.gov.uk/document.aspx?Document=EV02028_7073_FRP.pdf.

Mann, H.B., Whitney, D.R. (1947) 'On a test whether one of two random variables is stochastically larger than the other', The Annals of Mathematical Statistics, 50-60.

Margolis, J.D., Walsh, J.P. (2003) 'Misery loves companies: social initiatives by business', Administrative Science Quarterly, 48, 268-305.

Martinuzzi, A. (2011) 'Responsible Competitiveness: Linking CSR and Competitive Advantage in three European Industrial Sectors', in: Zeitschrift für Umweltpolitik und Umweltrecht/Journal of Environmental Policy and Law, Vol. 3/2011, pp. 297-337.

Martinuzzi, A., Krumay, B. (2013) 'The good, the bad and the successful: how CSR leads to competitive advantage and organizational transformation', Journal of Change Management, Vol. 13, Issue 4, pp. 424-443.

Martinuzzi, A., Kudlak, R., Faber, C., Wiman, A. (2011) 'CSR Activities and Impacts of the Textile Sector', RIMAS Working Papers, No. 2/2011, WU Vienna.

Matten, D., Moon J. (2008) '"Implicit" and "explicit" CSR: A conceptual framework for a comparative understanding of corporate social responsibility', Academy of Management Review, 33, 2, 404-24.

Mauro, P. (1995) 'Corruption and Growth', The Quarterly Journal of Economics, 110, 681–712.

Mauro, P. (1997) 'Corruption and the Global Economy. The effects of corruption on growth, investment and government expenditure: a cross-country analysis'. Available at http://www.adelinotorres.com/economia/Os%20efeitos%20da%20corrup%C3%A7%C3%A3o%20no%20mundo.pdf, Last accessed 08.01.2013.

Mayring, P. (2000) Qualitative Content Analysis, Forum Qualitative Social Research, 1, 2, Article 20.

McCrudden, C. (2004) 'Using public procurement to achieve social outcomes', Natural Resources Forum, 28, 4, 257-67.

OCED (2004) A new world map of textiles and clothing. OECD Publication, Paris, France.

McWilliams, A., Siegel, D. (2001) 'Corporate social responsibility: A theory of the firm perspective', Academy of Management Review, 26, 117-127.

De Mello, L. (1999) 'Foreign direct investment-led growth: evidence from time series and panel data', Oxford Economic Papers, 51, 133–151, http://web.ku.edu/~intecon/Courses/Econ915/papers/FDI_panel.pdf.

Michalski, R., Grobelny, J. (2007) 'Computer-aided subjective assessment of factors disturbing the occupational human performance', Occupational Ergonomics, 7, 27–42.

Miles, R. E., Snow, C.C. (1984) 'Fit, failure, and the hall of fame', California Management Review, 26, 10-28.

Mintzberg, H. (1979) 'Patterns in strategy formation', International Studies of Management & Organization, 9, 3, 67-86.

Moore, L. L., De Silva, I., & Hartmann, S. (2012) 'An Investigation into the Financial Return on Corporate Social Responsibility in the Apparel Industry', Journal of Corporate Citizenship, 2012, 45, 104-122.

Müller-Christ, G., Gandenberger S. (2006) 'Sustainable Resource Management: illustrated at the Problems of German Textile Industry', Proceedings IFSAM VIIIth World Congress, Berlin, Paper 00578, http://www.ctw-congress.de/ifsam/proceedings.html)=?.

Negandhi, A.R., Reimann, B.C. (1972) 'A contingency theory of organization re-examined in the context of a developing country', Academy of Management Journal, 15, 2, 137-146.

Nordas, H.K. (2004) 'The global textile and clothing industry post the agreement on textiles and clothing', Discussion paper No. 5, World Trade Organization.

OCED (2004) 'A new world map of textiles and clothing'. OECD Publication, Paris, France.

OECD (2011) OECD Science, Technology and Industry Scoreboard. OECD Publishing.

ODI (2011) 'Taking responsibility for complexity. How implementation can achieve results in the face of complex problems', ODI Working Paper 330, London.

Overeem, P., Peepercamp, M. (2012) 'Bonded (child) labour in the Indian garment industry', SOMO Institute, Netherlands.

Pearce, D.W., Markandya, A., Barbier, E.B. (1989) 'Blueprint for a green economy', EarthScan, London.

Pennings, J.M. (1975) 'The relevance of the structural-contingency model for organizational effectiveness', Administrative Science Quarterly, 20, 3, 393-410.

Pezzey, J. (1992) 'Sustainability: An interdisciplinary guide', Environmental Values, 1, 321-62.

Porter, M. E., Kramer M.R. (2011) 'Creating shared value', Harvard Business Review, 89, 2, 62-77.

Porter, M.E. (1976) 'Please note location of nearest exit: Exit barriers and planning', California Management Review, 19, 2, 21-33.

Prahalad, C. K. (2010) 'The fortune at the bottom of the pyramid: Eradicating poverty through profits', Dorling Kindersley Pvt Ltd, Wharton.

Preuss, L. (2009) 'Addressing sustainable development through public procurement: the case of local government', Supply Chain Management: An International Journal, 14, 3, 213-223.

Rahbek-Nielsen, E., Gwozdz, W., Hvass, K. (2013) 'Business model innovation, corporate sustainability and organizational values: Evidence from the Swedish fashion industry', CBS, Center for Corporate Social Responsibility, Working Paper.

Robeco, Booz & Co., (2008) 'Responsible Investing: A Paradigm Shift, From Niche to Mainstream', http://www.booz.com/media/file/Responsible-Investing-Paradigm-Shift.pdf.

Rumelt, R. P. (1974) 'Strategy, structure, and economic performance', Harvard Business School, Division of Research, Boston.

Schmitt, J., & Renken, U. (2012) 'How to Earn Money by Doing Good!: Shared Value in the Apparel Industry', Journal of Corporate Citizenship, 45.

Seelos, C., Mair, J. (2005) 'Social entrepreneurship: Creating new business models to serve the poor', Business Horizons, 48, 3, 241-46.

Shafer, S.M., Smith, H.J., Linder, J.C. (2005) 'The power of business models', Business Horizons, 48, 3, 199-207.

Sheehan, K. B. (2001). E-mail survey response rates: A review. Journal of Computer-Mediated Communication, 6(2), doi: 10.1111/j.1083-6101.2001.tb00117.x

Siegel, D.S., Vitaliano, D.F. (2007) 'An empirical analysis of the strategic use of corporate social responsibility', Journal of Economics & Management Strategy, 16, 3, 773-92.

Sparkes, R., Cowton, C. J. (2004) 'The maturing of socially responsible investment: a review of the developing link with corporate social responsibility', Journal of Business Ethics, 52, 1, 45-57.

Steurer, R. (2010) 'The role of governments in corporate social responsibility: characterising public policies on CSR in Europe', Policy Science, 43, 49-72.

Steurer, R., Berger, G., Konrad, A., Martinuzzi, A. (2007) 'Sustainable public procurement in EU member states: Overview of government initiatives and selected cases. Final Report to the EU High-Level Group on CSR', European Commission, Brussels.

Steurer, R., Martinuzzi, A., Margula, S. (2012) 'Public policies on CSR in Europe: Themes, instruments, and regional differences', Corporate Social Responsibility and Environmental Management, X,19, 206-227.

Stubbs, W., Cocklin, C. (2008) 'Conceptualizing a "Sustainability Business Model"', Organization and Environment, 21, 2, 103-127.

Surroca, J., Tribó, J., Waddock, S. (2010) 'Corporate responsibility and financial performance: the role of intangible resources', Strategic Management Journal, 31, 5, 463-490.

Tan J., Tan, D. (2005) 'Environment-strategy co-evolution and co-alignment: A staged model of Chinese SOEs under transition', Strategic Management Journal, 26, 2, 141-157.

Taplin, I.M. (2006) 'Restructuring and reconfiguration. The EU textile and clothing industry adapts to change', European Business Review, 18, 3, 172-186.

Taplin, I.M., Winterton, J. (2004) 'The European clothing industry. Meeting the competitive challenge', Journal of Fashion Marketing and Management, 8, 3, 256-261.

Teece, D. J. (2010) 'Business models, business strategy and innovation', Long Range Planning, 43, 2, 172-194.

Thrane, M., Johansen, H., Jakobsen, L. (2006) 'Corporate Social Responsibility: A New Tool in Development Aid', In: Corporate Citizenship in Development Countries: New Partnership Perspectives, by Esben Rahbek Pedersen and Mahad Huniche, 179-203. Copenhagen: Copenhagen Business School Press.

Titscher, S., Wodak, R., Meyer, M., Vetter, E. (1998) 'Methoden der Textanalyse', Leitfaden und Überblick, Opladen, Westdeutscher Verlag.

Van Marrewijk, M. (2003) 'Concepts and definitions of CSR and corporate sustainability: Between agency and communion', Journal of Business Ethics, 44, 95-105.

Welford R., Frost, S. (2006) 'Corporate social responsibility in Asian supply chains', Corporate Social Responsibility and Environmental Management, 13, 3, 166–176.

Williamson, C. (2010) 'Exploring the failure of foreign aid: The role of incentives and information', The Review of Austrian Economics, 23, 1, 17-33.

Yip, G.S. (1982) 'Diversification entry: Internal development versus acquisition', Strategic Management Journal, 3, 331-345.

Yunus, M., Moingeon, B., Lehmann-Ortega, L. (2010) 'Building social business models: Lessons from the Grameen experience', Long Range Planning, 43, 2-3, 308-25.

The Journal of Corporate Citizenship Issue 57 *March 2015*

DOI: [10.9774/GLEAF.5001.2015.ma.00004]

Apparel Manufacturers and the Business Case for Social Sustainability

'World Class' CSR and Business Model Innovation

Marsha A. Dickson and Rita K. Chang
University of Delaware, USA

Since the mid-1990s when major apparel brands began monitoring factories in their supply chains for adherence to codes of conduct regarding labour standards and working conditions, a 'cat and mouse' relationship between buyers and their suppliers has developed. Rather than proactively engaging in new business practices that would ensure safer, healthier, and fairer workplaces, many apparel manufacturers used deceptive and defensive practices to do as little as possible. This is beginning to change, however, as we have observed some apparel manufacturers who are key suppliers for global apparel brands beginning to proactively institute 'world class' corporate social responsibility (CSR). The purpose of this study was to describe the CSR work being carried out and to evaluate whether it creates a business case for social sustainability. We interviewed 18 CSR professionals whose companies buy from these manufacturers or whose organisations provide support for leadership activities of these manufacturers and conducted inductive and deductive analyses on the qualitative data. While the practices of these manufacturers have been notable, they have largely been unrewarded. Furthermore, they represent only business model improvements and expanded efforts will be needed to transform the working conditions for employees who toil in their facilities.

- Business model innovation
- Apparel industry
- Corporate social responsibility
- CSR
- Sustainability
- Qualitative research

Dr **Marsha A. Dickson** is Irma Ayers Professor of Human Services and co-director of the Sustainable Apparel Initiative at the University of Delaware. Dr Dickson has conducted research on social responsibility in the apparel industry in China, Guatemala, Hong Kong, India, Nicaragua, Thailand, and Vietnam. Dickson is a member of the board of directors of the Fair Labor Association (FLA), a non-governmental organisation originally formed by President Clinton to improve working conditions in factories around the world. She is also on the board of directors of the Fair Factories Clearinghouse. Dr Dickson has received several awards for her academic and industry contributions in social responsibility.

Fashion and Apparel Studies, University of Delaware, 211 Alison Hall West, Newark, DE 19716, USA

302-831-4475

Dickson@udel.edu

Rita Chang holds a Bachelor's Degree from the University of Delaware, where she created her own major, 'Social Responsibility in the Textile & Apparel Industry', and completed the UD Graduate Certificate in Socially Responsible & Sustainable Apparel Business. She participated in this research as part of her honours thesis. In 2010, Ms Chang moved to Taiwan to work in Nike, Inc.'s Considered Design team, where she managed a pilot project on the traceability of sustainable materials and was Vendor Capability Development Specialist in the Sustainable Manufacturing & Sourcing team building capacity internally and with Nike's suppliers to engage in sustainability initiatives. She then spent five months working as a sustainability and business consultant for Tiong Liong Industrial Co., Ltd, a major innovation-textile manufacturer in Taiwan. Ms Chang is currently pursuing an MBA with concentrations in Strategic Management and Environmental & Risk Management at the Wharton School of Business at the University of Pennsylvania.

✉ Fashion and Apparel Studies, University of Delaware, 211 Alison Hall West, Newark, DE 19716, USA

🖳 rkchangudel@gmail.com

The Journal of Corporate Citizenship Issue 57 *March 2015* © Greenleaf Publishing 2015

SINCE THE MID-1990S WHEN MAJOR apparel brands began monitoring factories in their supply chains for adherence to codes of conduct regarding labour standards and working conditions, a 'cat and mouse' relationship between buyers and their suppliers has developed. Rather than proactively engaging in new business practices that would ensure safer, healthier, and fairer workplaces, many apparel manufacturers used deceptive and defensive practices to do as little as possible, taking a minimal compliance and risk-management approach to sustainability (Dickson *et al.*, 2009). This is beginning to change, however, as we have observed some apparel manufacturers who are key suppliers for global apparel brands beginning to proactively institute corporate social responsibility (CSR) practices. CSR activities are pursued in efforts to achieve social sustainability, via improved labour standards and working conditions at facilities (Dickson *et al.*, 2009). Do the efforts of these leading apparel manufacturers reflect business model innovation for social sustainability? CSR professionals whose companies buy from these manufacturers or whose organisations provide support for leadership activities of the manufacturers are in a unique position to provide empirical observations about the work from which the extent of innovation can be evaluated.

Business models broadly describe the ways in which businesses organise to deliver value to customers and profitably distribute the value (Baden-Fuller and Morgan, 2010). Teece (2010) noted that business models explain:

> the manner by which the enterprise delivers value to customers, entices customers to pay for value, and converts those payments to profit. It thus reflects management's hypothesis about what customers want, how they want it, and how the enterprise can organize to best meet those needs, get paid for doing so, and make a profit (p. 172).

Elements of business models involve the key decisions that are made, when, by whom, and why (Girotra and Netessine, 2013). Although business models are highly situational, not 'one size fits all' (Kiron *et al.*, 2013a; Teece, 2010), they can be used to classify and compare businesses (Teece, 2010). Additionally, ideal models can be developed from exemplary cases and then be used to guide other businesses in innovating their own new models (Baden-Fuller and Morgan, 2010; Teece, 2010). Business model innovation is increasingly viewed as a critical component of sustainability (Kiron *et al.*, 2013a).

The twofold purpose of this study was to: 1) describe the CSR work being carried out by apparel manufacturers that are viewed within the industry as 'world class' in these efforts; and 2) evaluate whether that work creates a business case for social sustainability. 'World class' is a term that has been used in research to describe business effectiveness and competitiveness in manufacturing (e.g. Eid, 2009; Talebi *et al.*, 2014; Tarzijan, 2013). It was also referenced in an analysis of company codes of conduct and the principles they contain (Paine *et al.*, 2005). This study appears to be the first to apply the concept of 'world class' to the work carried out by manufacturers to achieve competitive and effective social sustainability.

We focused on manufacturer efforts to assure workers in their facilities were provided their rights indicated by the International Labour Organization's

Fundamental Principles and Rights at Work addressing the abolition of child and forced labour and discriminatory labour practices, and additional conventions addressing wages, hours of work and others. The rights are routinely addressed in the codes of conduct apparel brands expect their manufacturers to follow (Dickson et al., 2009). We did not focus on efforts taken to protect the environment beyond the health and safety impacts of environmental pollutants and hazards. In talking with CSR executives, we operationalised 'world class' as the ideal/best CSR work carried out by apparel manufacturers to assure that workers' rights are met.

The United Nations Guiding Principles assert that every company, no matter where it is located or its size, has a responsibility to respect workers' rights by ascertaining that the company's practices do not directly or indirectly interfere. The Guiding Principles recognise that work toward respect of workers' rights will require ongoing commitment (United Nations, 2011). The research is unique not only for its focus on business model innovation, but also for its focus on apparel manufacturers. Most research on CSR practices in the apparel industry has focused on the efforts of well-known brands and retailers rather than the less well-known companies that manufacture their products and are critical to improved social sustainability.[1]

We tapped the insights and experiences of 18 CSR professionals about the work being carried out by apparel manufacturers for improved social sustainability. The research sheds light on elements of an improved business model that is emerging. The research also points to additional changes that will be necessary to transform apparel manufacturing to greater levels of social sustainability.

Sustainability and business model innovation

We used Schaltegger et al.'s (2011) Integrated Framework of Sustainability Strategy, Business Drivers, and Business Model Innovation as a conceptual framework for our study. The Integrated Framework suggests that the degree of business model innovation is determined by a manufacturer's response to core business case drivers, via their sustainability strategy and business model pillars. Depending on how extensively the manufacturer innovates its business model there is a certain level of business case for sustainability. Being profitable is a basic component of a successful business model; therefore, manufacturing with a business case for sustainability would be profitable. Beyond simply improved profitability, Schaltegger et al. (2011) consider a broad range of business case drivers that can be addressed to create a business case for sustainability. To fully realise the potential business case, sustainability strategies are linked to significant changes in the business model.

---

[1] Dickson (2013) provides an in-depth review of literature researching CSR practices of apparel brands and retailers.

Recently there has been a flurry of scholarly publications conceptualising and reporting empirical research about business model innovation for sustainability. Researchers have proposed various business model elements that should be studied, including what decisions and changes are made, when the decisions and changes are made, how decisions and models are changed, by whom, and why (Girotra and Netessine, 2013; Kiron et al., 2013a; Zollo et al., 2013). The ideas from the literature are organised as they relate to Schaltegger et al.'s (2011) business model pillars, business case drivers, and sustainability strategy.

Business model pillars

According to Schaltegger et al. (2011), the pillars of a business model are determinant factors in achieving profits and a business case for sustainability. The four pillars are value proposition, customer relationships, business infrastructure, and financial aspects; they are not mutually exclusive. Value proposition is associated with the products and services offered for which customers are willing to pay (Schaltegger et al., 2011). An essential element of the value proposition involves what a company makes and for whom (Girotra and Netessine, 2013; Kiron et al., 2013a), such as niche product for a high-end buyer. The pillar emphasising customer relationships differs from the value proposition by emphasising the relationship (and long-term revenue) created from satisfying customer demands, including continuously satisfying quality and delivery requirements. Business infrastructure encompasses the internal resources and value chain network needed to improve customer relationships and deliver value and may include vertical integration of portions of the supply chain. The financial aspects business model pillar relates to reductions to costs and optimising revenue (Schaltegger et al., 2011).

Business case drivers

Business case drivers for sustainability motivate the changes a company will consider and implement. Drivers of business model change can be influenced by external competitors and stakeholders and by internal motivations and aspirations (Zollo et al., 2013). Schaltegger et al. (2011) include the following as business case drivers.

▶ Costs and risks

▶ Sales and profits

▶ Reputational or brand value

▶ Attractiveness as an employer

▶ Innovative capabilities

It is possible to analyse social sustainability activities in relationship to these drivers, determining *why* innovations in a business model are pursued or why they are not. Manufacturers hoping to receive an order from Walmart will almost certainly aim to reduce costs, but may also hope to increase the volume of sales as a result.

Some companies hope to develop a brand that stands out among competitors for social and environmental sustainability that meets customers' demands (Tollin and Vej, 2013) and thus enhance reputational and brand value. Patagonia has developed a reputation for sustainable products and as an attractive place for employment.[2] Market creation can expand sales and includes efforts associated with sustainability that involve innovation in both products and business models whereby new customers in emerging markets are pursued with new product development or by extending supply chain networks (Tollin and Vej, 2013). Nike emphasises innovation not only with its products, but also its sustainability efforts.[3]

The pressure for business legitimisation influences how companies deliver value over time through their evolving objectives, systems, and processes and is associated with the reduction of risks driver. Under external pressure for business legitimisation, such as with government regulation or strong customer or other stakeholder demands, companies tend to adopt common sustainability standards, which constrain innovation in products and processes (Zollo *et al.*, 2013) and may be counter-productive to enhancing innovative capabilities.

Furthermore, pursuing new markets, reducing risks by adopting standards needed for business legitimisation, and delivering the value customers demand is inadequate to fully support the business case for sustainability. Companies must also create the ability to *capture* value or profit from the business model innovation. Innovation is more likely to occur when customers prefer sustainable products or services *and are willing to pay extra for these* (Kiron *et al.*, 2013b). Incentives provided by customers might include paying for desired sustainability-related services, extending contracts, and creating long-term partnerships that 'align the incentive horizon of suppliers and buyers' and facilitate long-term investments that hold risk (Girotra and Netessine, 2013). Yet, the research on business models and sustainability has neglected the role of uncertainty, risks, decisions, and incentives in driving business model innovation for sustainability (Girotra and Netessine, 2013).

Sustainability strategy

Business strategy for sustainability involves identifying, creating, and strengthening links between economic, social, and environmental activities. As social and environmental issues become increasingly relevant to strategy, it is likely that a company makes more extensive modifications to its business model or even develops a new model (Schaltegger *et al.*, 2011). Literature on business model innovation for sustainability has considered a variety of management systems and processes, business resources and structures, and beliefs and

---

2 Personal communications, Nicole Bassett, June 2010
3 http://nikeinc.com/pages/responsibility

values, along with how they are integrated, organised, and leveraged through value chains to create strategies for delivering the value proposition (Kiron *et al.*, 2013a; Tollin and Vej, 2013; Zollo *et al.*, 2013). New systems and tools may be created to analyse and report to stakeholders about sustainability work (Tollin and Vej, 2013). For manufacturing firms integrating environmental sustainability activities across their general management functions, including health and safety, quality, and strategy, those innovating their *processes* achieved better environmental performance, whereas those embracing *product* innovation achieved better economic performance (Hall and Wagner, 2012).

From the perspective of Zollo *et al.* (2013), changing business model structures and systems involves initiatives associated with strategising, expanding capabilities, organising, and enhancing relationship quality. Supply chain innovation includes establishment of relationships with non-governmental organisations (NGOs) and other stakeholders in ensuring a continuous supply of necessary raw materials (Tollin and Vej, 2013). The availability of information often determines when decisions are made. Business decisions made in pursuit of sustainability may require risky investments based on incomplete information that has the potential to restrain company profits. Innovation could be achieved by changing the timing or sequence of decisions (Girotra and Netessine, 2013).

Further complicating changes to sustainability strategy is the fact that business decisions with sustainability implications are often made by individuals whose interests and incentives diverge or conflict with others in a value chain (Girotra and Netessine, 2013). Working to develop shared commitment and understanding of sustainability within the company and with supply chain partners can support business model innovations (Tollin and Vej, 2013). Dickson *et al.* (2009) have noted the need for alignment among those within company CSR and procurement divisions so that consistent expectations are set for suppliers. Furthermore, changing the actual decision maker can improve sustainability performance, such as when suppliers are empowered to make decisions related to products and processes (Girotra and Netessine, 2013). Simply put, business model innovation for sustainability should 'empower the right decision makers with the best available information and value-creating incentives to make the right decisions with measurable consequences' (Girotra and Netessine, 2013).

The sustainability strategy of a company comprises its sustainability activities, which could be defensive, accommodative, or proactive (Schaltegger *et al.*, 2011). Defensive strategies reflect limited integration often in reaction to perceived cost-constraints. Defensive strategies involve managers approaching sustainability in narrow and reactive ways, minimally complying with buyers' requests and legal requirements in hopes of reducing risks and protecting existing sales (Schaltegger *et al.*, 2011). The deceptive practices described in the opening paragraph of this paper reflect defensive strategies that apparel manufacturers pursued over the years in response to brands' and retailers' monitoring and remediation efforts. The prevalence of double and even triple or quadruple books, coaching workers to lie to auditors, and hiding production at sub-contracted facilities with poor working conditions are examples (Dickson et al., 2009). Defensive sustainability strategies protect the existing business model or involve only adjustment or adoption; they do not create a long-term business case for sustainability (Schaltegger et al., 2011).

The accommodative strategy reflects fuller integration of sustainability into the business, but still a fairly cautious adjustment to internal processes; consideration of social and environmental issues is modest. Management may use systems and tools for organisational control, and recognise that they need to change the organisation and train employees. Examples might be companies that have implemented lean manufacturing technology at the insistence of their buyers, or ones that have developed a CSR programme that addresses the issues of importance to brands and retailers. The existing business model may have some changes and is improved. The accommodative strategy addresses some of the drivers supporting a business case (Schaltegger et al., 2011).

On the other hand, proactive sustainability strategies reflect full integration of social and environmental goals where pursuing them becomes part of the core business of the manufacturer and a new value proposition is created. All of a company's business processes are adapted towards sustainability goals as the business model is redesigned. Businesses pursuing a proactive strategy strive for business leadership with strong sustainability performance and achieve the business case for sustainability by strongly and continuously addressing many of the business case drivers (Schaltegger et al., 2011). Patagonia's mission places sustainability at the heart of its business and the company has helped found the Sustainable Apparel Coalition (Chouinard et al., 2011), is an accredited member of the Fair Labor Association (www.fairlabor.org), and has been one of the first to have production in a fair trade certified factory (https://www.patagonia.com).

Degree of business model innovation

Together, the business case drivers, business model pillars, and sustainability strategy allow for an assessment of the degree of business model innovation. The four degrees of adjustment, adoption, improvement, and redesign reflect the extent that changes are made to the original business model pillars and the breadth of response to various business case drivers. Adjustment means that only one element of the business model is changed or only minor changes to a few elements are made and the value proposition is excluded from changes. Adoption reflects changes that are made primarily to match the value propositions of competitors. This may involve changes to product and services, and perhaps to customer relationships and business infrastructure. Improvement of the business model involves changes to most of the business elements but retention of the same general value proposition. Redesign, however, regards changes that result in an entirely new value proposition (Schaltegger et al., 2011).

This research sought to understand the extent to which business model innovation is occurring within leading apparel manufacturers and determine whether it provides them a business case for pursuing their CSR work and social sustainability goals. If a business case for sustainability exists, the innovation may reflect an ideal business model that would provide an example for other apparel manufacturers to follow, thus transforming the conditions for workers toiling in global supply chains. The businesses we considered in our study are manufacturers of apparel—the actual businesses that make products bound for the stores of global brands and retailers.

Methods

During 2009 and 2010, we interviewed 18 CSR executives of large and well-known brands and retailers based in the United States and Europe, and of consulting/auditing businesses working globally with apparel manufacturers on improving social sustainability. These executives are uniquely positioned to provide information about world class CSR work; collectively their companies collaborate with thousands of factories globally. During in-depth interviews conducted by telephone or Skype, CSR executives were asked to describe the characteristics and practices they had observed or expected at world class levels of CSR performance. Additionally, the executives were asked how improved social sustainability was being rewarded, and whether a competitive advantage existed for world class CSR. Interviews ranged from 40 to 100 minutes and were audio recorded; verbatim transcripts were created from the recordings.

The qualitative data were analysed by two researchers using the constant comparative method to inductively generate themes reflecting world class CSR practices and characteristics (see Strauss and Corbin, 1998). A second phase of data analysis involved deductively coding the data for connections the CSR executives made with business model pillars and business case drivers. Business model innovation can be determined by a manufacturers' response to core drivers, via their sustainability strategy and business model pillars. Based on the findings, we interpreted the types of sustainability strategies being pursued and the extent of business model innovation. Frequencies with which the 18 CSR executives mentioned content relevant to the various coding categories are reported.

Results

CSR executives described a number of business characteristics and CSR practices that world class apparel manufacturers have and carry out in efforts to improve social sustainability (see Table 1). The most frequently mentioned coding categories reflected practices carried out by the business. Having management systems provides consistency to business practices and controls the negative impacts a manufacturer may have on working conditions and labour standards, as well as all other areas of the business (i.e. production, human resource management). Management systems were mentioned by all respondents and related to not just having policies in place, but also implementing them and tracking performance. One CSR executive described the role of management systems as follows.

> First and foremost, you know, CSR in these factories is actually good management. So, you know, we have socially responsible factories that have qualified health and safety engineers on staff and who have set up systems to make sure that safety standards that are issued from the head office actually kind of trace to the work floor. You know, they have grievance procedures. So, you know, I hesitate to even call this social responsibility. This is just basic common sense, good management.

Table 1 Business characteristics and CSR practices of 'world class' apparel manufacturers

Characteristics/ Practices	Description	Frequency (n=18)
Management systems	Having management systems in place for CSR and all other areas of the business (e.g. production, HR); includes policies, implementation, follow up, correction, etc.	18
Taking ownership of CSR	Taking initiative and responsibility for having own programme, finding problems and fixing them; accountable	17
Focused on workers	Empowering workers, involving them, communicating with them, seeing them as critically important to the business; good grievance systems; worker committees; attentive to cultural and physical needs; may involve training to enhance skills, prevision of benefits, making workers happy, paying them well	16
Open, transparent, trustworthy, and honest	Not afraid to share the issues they have with their buyers; not hiding issues	16
CSR staff or committee	People with responsibility for CSR that carry out activities/ internal auditing to assess compliance/effectiveness of CSR programme; staff/committee might be separate from or integrated into HR/other functions	15
Owner and management commitment and values	The commitment and values of management, owners, and top leadership; changes in management attitudes as a result of various incidents or experiences (e.g. grad school in the US); a shift in mind-set	14
Profits and reinvestments into CSR activities	Reinvests in the company	14
CSR, both social and environmental	Compatibility between addressing social and environmental issues	13
Strong management	Trained/highly qualified professional managers and line supervisors; people with appropriate technical skills (e.g. engineers); motivated management	12

Characteristics/ Practices	Description	Frequency (n=18)
Engage with stakeholders	Seeking collaboration/assistance from groups beyond buyers where relevant (e.g. emergency planning, addressing child labour); communicating with stakeholders. Depending on the issues, stakeholders might be government, trade associations, NGOs, multistakeholder initiatives, others	11
Community focused	Being aware of broader community impacts; caring about and trying to do something for the local community; philanthropy and investing in the broader community; programmes to help workers and their families beyond the factory needs	11
Larger firms	Including larger factories, larger factory groups, multinational manufacturers	11
Adhere to government legislation	Following host country laws	10
Good relationship with brand	Long term relationships with brands marked by reasonable expectations and support in achieving those; collaborative, sufficient dialogue with buyers	10
Public CSR reports	Gathers and reports data on effectiveness of CSR work; shares publicly problems they are having; provides information publicly so others can learn from their successes	10
Visionary and strategic	Forward thinking; strategic plans; often involving top leadership (owner/manager) of company	10
Compliant with standards	General compliance with internationally recognised labour standards or management systems certification programmes (e.g. SA8000, ISO systems)	10
Government-supported	Incentivised and supported by government through regulation and enforcement of laws, and broader initiatives in support of workers (e.g. ILO Better Work)	10
Dynamic	Ever-increasing demands for CSR; making progress toward compliance with continuous improvement	8
Capacity building	Training and capacity building of managers and workers; part of effective management systems	7
Buyers with high expectations	Responsive to rigorous expectations of their buyers; do not produce for buyers that close their eyes to the problems	5
Effective multinationally	CSR programmes are effective in all countries of operation	4
Based in North Asia	China, Taiwan, etc.	4
Produce high end merchandise	Produce higher end products, products with higher price points, not producing for discounters	3
Vertically integrated	Also owns mills, cotton, etc.	3

Taking ownership for CSR was mentioned by 94% of CSR executives and this involved proactively taking responsibility for identifying internal problems affecting workers and being accountable for remediating them. A focus on workers was mentioned by 89% of CSR executives who expected world class apparel manufacturers to involve workers in identifying and resolving problems through strong communications programmes, including grievance systems, and programmes that empower them. A focus on workers involves 'management acknowledging the value that the workers bring'.

Having staff with responsibility for CSR and who carry out activities such as internal auditing and assessing effectiveness of the CSR programme was mentioned by 83% of executives. Being open in sharing the issues they face in attempting to improve social sustainability, especially in contrast to hiding those problems, was mentioned by 89% of executives who valued transparency as a characteristic of world class CSR. For example, one executive described world class apparel manufacturers as those...

> ...that wouldn't be afraid to share some of their issues with us. Quite honestly if a factory is not reporting some of their issues to you whether it be in their manufacturing, their quality, or even compliance, then...you're just not finding out about it. It's not that it doesn't exist, so I think that's quite important.

In describing the characteristics and CSR practices of world class apparel manufacturers, the executives interviewed noted that the commitment and values of owners and top management were essential as was being a profitable company able to reinvest for improved social sustainability (78%). Seventy-two per cent of respondents believed that apparel manufacturers with world class programmes addressed both the social and environmental aspects of sustainability in their work.

Additional characteristics and practices mentioned by the CSR executives are reported in Table 1. It should be noted that beyond being profitable and having executive-level commitment, there was much less agreement on other characteristics of world class manufacturers such as location, size and scope of operations, or the types of merchandise they produced.

Driven by increased sales and reduced costs

The content of the interviews with CSR executives provided insight about the business case drivers apparel manufacturers were addressing with world class CSR programmes (see Table 2). In observing what motivates apparel manufacturers to take leadership in CSR, by far the most dominant theme, reported by 89% of respondents, related to the sales and profits pillar and primarily dealt with hopes for increasing orders. However, some noted that manufacturers were hoping to retain the orders they had as other factors of production, particularly wages, decreased their competitive advantages. As one executive explained, 'They're chasing the money and unless we can show them the money, they're not really all that interested'.

Sixty-seven per cent of respondents connected world class CSR with costs and cost reduction, involving adopting more efficient and 'lean' production methods, increasing productivity, and generally becoming more efficient. Efforts associated with reputation and brand value were noted by 56% of CSR executives who often cited the efforts of particular companies or of the industries in certain countries to promote themselves as 'ahead of the curve' in social sustainability and improve their image in the eyes of their customers. Half of the respondents mentioned that CSR work addressed attractiveness as an employer because it improved the atmosphere and morale of the factory, reduced absenteeism, and increased employee retention.

Table 2 Business case drivers addressed in world class social sustainability

Driver	Frequency (n=18)
Sales and profit margin	16
Costs and cost reduction	12
Reputation and brand value	10
Attractiveness as employer	9
Risk and risk reduction	6
Innovative capabilities	3

When content associated with risk and risk reduction was mentioned, it often indicated the apparel manufacturers' efforts to lessen their risk to the buyer in terms of the possibility of high-profile non-compliance with their codes of conduct or volatile worker unrest. CSR executives noted that because of reputational risks, world class manufacturers were more likely to produce for high-profile brands, such as Nike, adidas, Gap, and Polo Ralph Lauren. The small number of CSR executives describing apparel manufacturers in ways indicative of improving their innovative capabilities did so by discussing the manufacturers' research and development efforts and long-term strategic planning.

Improving customer relationships and the value proposition

CSR executives most heavily focused on two business pillars of a business model when discussing the CSR work of world class apparel manufacturers. As seen in Table 3, nearly all executives (94%) connected world class CSR work with customer relationships; it involved manufacturers making efforts to meet the needs of their customers. For example, one executive stated that...

> ...the world class leaders...time and time again have been able to prove to the customers that they're dependable. You could always get it cheaper, but if you want it done right, if you want it done consistently, if you want to make sure that the product is in the stores, and if you don't have any compliance issue, you go with me. If you want to just do it cheaper, you don't go with me. You go with someone else.

Table 3 Business model pillars addressed in world class social sustainability

Pillar	Frequency (n=18)
Customer relationships	17
Value proposition	14
Financial aspects	10
Business infrastructure	4

Connections of world class CSR with the apparel manufacturers' value proposition were noted by 78% of the executives interviewed. Content under this category related to proactively making CSR part of the company's core business and being known as the best in the industry at CSR in addition to improving positioning in the market. As explained by one executive, 'A world-class socially responsible [manufacturer] would be one that really wants to incorporate CSR, or improving conditions...the ones who really want to embrace and embed that into their business model'.

The financial aspects business model pillar was mentioned by 56% of the CSR executives interviewed and their comments were often associated with the reduction of costs through increased efficiency and productivity.

An accommodative sustainability strategy

Management systems and processes, tools, business resources and structures, and beliefs and values regarding social issues contribute to a company's sustainability strategy (Kiron *et al.*, 2013a; Tollin and Vej, 2013; Zollo *et al.*, 2013). While we observed some evidence of defensive and proactive strategies, by and large the practices and characteristics described as part of world class CSR programmes, and the business case drivers those address, suggest world class apparel manufacturers are implementing an accommodative sustainability strategy that is heavily focused on responsiveness to their customers. World class apparel manufacturers are taking ownership of CSR and implementing management systems, utilising CSR staff and strong management with the support of their top management. In doing so, they are hoping to increase sales and improve their relationships with customers by being open and transparent and reducing the risks of negative publicity. Furthermore, they are addressing the financial aspects of their businesses by focusing on increased efficiency and reduced costs. Increased focused on workers enhances the manufacturers' attractiveness as employers and their business infrastructure. One executive summed up the accommodative efforts by explaining,

> They're responding to what the customers are asking for. I've seen factories that are taking initiative to improve their workers' lives beyond what the clients are asking for, but most of them aren't. And so if you are looking at world class the way the world is today, I think you'd have to say that a world-class factory, it's all internally based. And so they're striving to set up systems within the factories you know. To be responsive to the workers in terms of making sure everybody gets paid and [to assure] health and safety.

We begin to see more evidence of a proactive sustainability strategy when considering the less frequently cited practices of engagement with stakeholders and taking a community focus, which would build the business infrastructure and further increase attractiveness as an employer. Several executives mentioned companies in Sri Lanka, such as MAS Holdings, that were investing in their communities and green factories. Additionally, when combined with owner and top management's commitment and values and the reinvestment of profits into the company's CSR activities, being visionary and strategic could enhance the sales and reputation of world class apparel manufacturers in ways that further expand their value propositions. Some manufacturers described as being world class were pursuing non-sustainability focused innovation and strategy, such as the TAL Group based in Hong Kong which was highlighted for its product innovation as well as strong management systems. The Esquel Group, also of Hong Kong, was mentioned in terms of its visionary leadership and forward thinking CSR team.

Business model innovation constrained to improvements

Together, the business case drivers, business model pillars, and sustainability strategy allow for the assessment of the degree of business model innovation. The four degrees of adjustment, adoption, improvement, and redesign reflect the possible changes made to the original business model (Schaltegger et al., 2011). From those results, the degree of business model innovation evident among apparel manufacturers with world class CSR programmes is 'business model improvement'. While most of the business model pillars reflect some change, the heavy focus is on improving existing customer relationships, thus retaining generally the same value proposition. Focusing on the existing business model precludes business model redesign.

Discussion and conclusions

The purpose of this research was to describe the CSR work being carried out by apparel manufacturers that are viewed within the industry as 'world class' in their efforts and to evaluate whether that work creates a business case for social sustainability. Regarding the CSR programmes, practices and characteristics of world class apparel manufacturers, the executives interviewed described professionally managed businesses that have made extensive strides in addressing their customers' needs for improved working conditions and labour standards, reduced costs, and more transparent and open relationships. These findings extend the literature on CSR practices by focusing on the work of apparel manufacturers, not simply the well-known brands and retailers whose products they supply (Dickson, 2013).

Depending on how well apparel manufacturers innovate their business models, there may be a certain level of business case for sustainability. Based on the

CSR executive interviews, the primary business case drivers of the envisioned world class manufacturer were sales and profits and costs and cost reduction. The CSR executives described the world class manufacturer as one that would do what is necessary to keep revenue, while decreasing expenses. The business model pillars of such a manufacturer were customer relationship and value proposition, where the manufacturer is constantly addressing what can be done to satisfy the customer.

It is natural to assume that a world class socially sustainable manufacturer would have implemented significant changes to its business model and we heard of a few examples of companies that had combined sustainability with other types of innovation and visionary leadership. Yet, this study finds that the majority of CSR executives have only envisioned a manufacturer making slight improvements to the business model in response to their expectations. This stark difference in 'what could be' versus 'what should be' has wide implications, particularly in how customers may in effect be limiting their current manufacturing partners' vision of world class social responsibility and the potential for business success.

The viewpoints of most of the CSR executives indicate that current business model innovation is largely constrained to focus on buyer demands and customer relationships. This overemphasis on customers overshadows consideration of other stakeholders (i.e. communities, new markets) or internal aspirations that could fuel broader innovation needed for manufacturer business success. As a result, few manufacturers invest in new services and business models, and stretch to create a value proposition that meets their own internal needs and those of their broader stakeholders. Instead, manufacturers focus on 'What does my buyer want?' This situation is made worse with buyers who appear not to reward sustainability activities that would incentivise new approaches to business that provide competitive advantage. If buyers are unwilling to pay for world class CSR work, it fails a fundamental test of business model success (see Kiron et al., 2013b; Teece 2010). The business case for CSR plateaus when manufacturers meeting buyers' expectations continue to receive orders but do not receive higher prices, larger volumes, or longer contracts for those.

By the majority of CSR professionals inadvertently envisioning 'world class' socially sustainable manufacturers as only exhibiting business model improvement, it indicates the type of mindset and outlook buying companies currently have for social sustainability. As long as social sustainability is simply required by buyers as a minimum expectation for keeping their business, there may not be any business case for sustainability for manufacturers, especially when large investments are required or the buyer does not reward the activities. Apparel manufacturers may simply view extensive CSR work as too risky with uncertain benefits (Girotra and Netessine, 2013). If social sustainability continues to be primarily buyer-driven and solely an expectation for business legitimacy, then there is decreased relevance to manufacturers, decreased integration of sustainability in manufacturers' businesses, and ultimately, decreased business model innovation (see Zollo et al., 2013). In other words, in the CSR executives' current definition of world class CSR, the business case for social sustainability for manufacturers is largely unrealised. The fact that the envisioned world class manufacturer has only an accommodative sustainability strategy is another indicator that brands are limiting the potential of present day manufacturers.

Toward world class improvements for workers

The CSR expectations of customers of global apparel manufacturers have undoubtedly been influential in improving labour standards and working conditions in factories around the world. World class apparel manufacturers have responded to their customer concerns, but require further innovation to achieve business success and to more fully transform their business models for social sustainability. Going forward, it would be valuable to identify and research with in-depth case studies, manufacturers that have successfully implemented business model redesign to understand the possibilities and the effects on their relationships with buyers. Another approach would be to research the trending community-focus of socially sustainable manufacturers—given the large potential of manufacturers to positively impact their communities, what prevents them from taking action?

In order to reach a greater business case for sustainability, manufacturers need to embrace a proactive (not accommodative) sustainability strategy, accompanied with broader business model innovation. The manufacturer would have to make their business more than just about money and profits, and make sustainability part of their core system. The manufacturer needs to better consider how social responsibility and sustainability can positively influence risk management, reputation and corporate brand value, attractiveness to employees, and innovation. The manufacturer might consider offering new services for its customers, whether it is proactively gathering data needed for traceability, management of second tier suppliers, or new partnerships with other companies to create recycling options, and other innovative ideas. To reach business model redesign, a manufacturer essentially needs to take advantage of itself—take advantage of the fact that it has the ability to make not just a better product, but a better employee, a better environment, and a better community. We urge their customers, major apparel brands and retailers, to empower their manufacturers to pursue broader innovations for their long-term success, and provide rewards and incentives for doing so.

References

Baden-Fuller, C. and Morgan, M.S. (2010), Business models as models. Long Range Planning, 43, 156-171.

Chouinard, Y., Ellison, J., and Ridgeway, R. (2011), 'The sustainable economy', Harvard Business Review, October, 52-62.

Dickson, M.A. (2013), 'Toward an integrated human rights-based approach to corporate social responsibility in the global apparel industry', Black, S. *et al.*, The Handbook of Fashion Studies, Bloomsbury, London.

Dickson, M.A., Loker, S., and Eckman, M. (2009), Social Responsibility in the Global Apparel Industry, Fairchild Books, New York.

Eid, R., (2009), 'Factors affecting success of world class manufacturing implementation in less developed countries', Journal of Manufacturing Technology and Management, 20, 2, 989–1008.

Girotra, K. and Netessine, S. (2013), 'Business model innovation for sustainability', INSEAD The Business School for the World [working paper]. Retrieved 8/26/13 at http://www.insead.edu/facultyresearch/research/doc.cfm?did=52400.

Hall, J. and Wagner, M. (2012), 'Integrating sustainability into firms' processes: Performance effects and the moderating role of business models and innovation', Business Strategy and the Environment, 21, 183-196.

Kiron, D., Kruschwitz, N., Haanaes, K., Reeves, M., and Goh, E. (2013a), 'The innovation bottom line: How companies that see sustainability as both necessary and an opportunity, and change their business models in response, are finding success', MIT Sloan Management Review and The Boston Consulting Group.

Kiron, D., Kruschwitz, N., Reeves, M. and Goh, E. (2013b), 'The benefits of sustainability-driven innovation.' MIT Sloan Management Review, 54, 2, 69-73.

Paine, L., Deshpande, R., Margolis, J.D., and Bettcher, K.E. (2005, December), 'Up to code: Does your company's conduct meet world-class standards?', Harvard Business Review, 122-133.

Schaltegger, S., Ludeke-Freund, F., and Hansen, E.G. (2011), 'Business cases for sustainability and the role of business model innovation: Developing a conceptual framework', Centre for Sustainability Management, Leuphana University of Lueneburg, Germany.

Strauss, A. and Corbin, J. (1998), Basics of Qualitative Research Techniques and Procedures for Developing Grounded Theory (2nd ed.), Thousand Oaks, CA, Sage.

Talebi, D., Farsijani, H., Sedighi, F., and Nikabadi, M.S. (2014), 'The role of quality bench-marking deployment to world-class manufacturing', Quality Engineering, 26, 2, 206-214.

Tarzijan, J. (2013), 'The emergence of world-class companies in Chile: Analysis of cases and a framework to assess integration decisions', Journal of Business Research, 66, 1728-1735.

Teece, D.J. (2010), 'Business models, business strategy and innovation', Long Range Planning, 43, 172-194.

Tollin, K. and Vej, J. (2013), 'Sustainability in business: Understanding meanings, triggers, and enablers', Journal of Strategic Marketing, 20, 7, 625-641.

United Nations (2011), 'Guiding principles on business and human rights', New York. Available at http://www.ohchr.org/Documents/Publications/GuidingPrinciplesBusinessHR_EN.pdf.

Zollo, M., Cennamo, C. and Neumann, K. (2013), 'Beyond what and why: Understanding evolution towards sustainable enterprise models', Organization & Environment, 26, 3, 241-259.

DOI: [10.9774/GLEAF.5001.2015.ma.00009]

'Plan A'

Analysing Business Model Innovation for Sustainable Consumption in Mass-Market Clothes Retailing*

Elizabeth Morgan
University of Leeds, UK

Mass-market retailers account for the majority of sales to consumers in developed markets and therefore have considerable influence on sustainable consumption. However, retailers' approaches and business model innovation for sustainable consumption, as described in their own reports, have rarely been investigated. The clothing sector has been identified as having huge environmental impacts, but is under-explored in terms of innovation for sustainability. This study develops a clothing 'Use Chain' and analyses the clothing initiatives within a well-known corporate responsibility programme from the UK's leading clothing retailer, Marks & Spencer's 'Plan A', in order to assess evidence for business model innovation. CSR reports were analysed across seven years, using a framework that integrates elements of the business case rationale with the identification of business model innovation. It finds evidence that Marks & Spencer had no initial plan for business model innovation, but over the period, it emerged from two of the initiatives, although not at systemic scale. It finds also that several of the initiatives were built on the business's sources of competitive advantage and therefore these would not necessarily be replicable by other firms. These findings suggest that, while leading firms may be capable of creating new sustainable business models, sector-level sustainable consumption may not necessarily follow. Nonetheless, the Use Chain has highlighted new opportunities for clothing businesses to innovate for sustainable consumption.

- Plan A
- Business model innovation
- Retailing
- Sustainable consumption
- Marks & Spencer

Elizabeth Morgan is a PhD researcher at the University of Leeds investigating business innovation for sustainability. She was previously Global Product Director for Boots, the UK's leading health and beauty retailer, where she initiated and led the Boots Centre for Innovation and, before that, Marketing Director for Carlsberg Tetley. Elizabeth is also a Trustee Director of the Energy Saving Trust, the UK's leading source of independent advice for consumers seeking to reduce energy and water use.

✉ School of Earth and Environment, University of Leeds, Leeds LS2 9JT, United Kingdom

🖳 ee09lm@leeds.ac.uk

* Thanks are due to Tim Foxon, Anne Tallontire, Kerli Kant Hvass, and two anonymous reviewers for their helpful comments on earlier versions of this paper.

C LOTHING IS AN IMPORTANT SYSTEM to be investigated for new insights into sustainable consumption. Sustainable consumption lacks a precise definition against which an individual or business can be assessed (Jackson, 2005) and is contested (Jackson, 2006). However, it encompasses ideas of intra-generational equity and planetary carrying capacity, similar to the equally contested field of sustainable development. Examples of these demand fourfold (von Weizsäcker et al., 1998) or tenfold (Wackernagel et al., 1997) improvement in output per unit of resource. If there is to be such transformational change in resource efficiency for sustainable consumption in developed countries, then retailing will need to transform. Large retailers are key actors; innovation in their business models will be necessary. While smaller companies can break new ground in sustainability, it is the large incumbent companies that have the scale to deliver significant impact (Hockerts and Wüstenhagen, 2010). Retailers as influencers of consumer behaviour in fashion and clothing have only recently been researched, and in limited contexts (Kozlowski et al., 2012).

In clothing, the consumer use phase has the largest environmental impact (Madsen et al., 2007; Allwood et al., 2006), yet this is a 'vastly under-explored area of innovation' (Fletcher, 2008: 76). This paper examines how the leading mass-market clothes retailer in the UK, Marks & Spencer (M&S), has sought to promote more environmentally sustainable consumer behaviour in clothing. The paper analyses M&S's business case drivers and business model innovation for eight initiatives about clothing use, employing Schaltegger et al.'s (2012) framework. The initiatives are selected from M&S's 'Plan A', a well-documented corporate responsibility programme. This analysis identifies the business case rationale for the activities and how they are linked to business model innovation. Drawing on this, the paper considers implications for the study of business model innovation for sustainability and system level innovation, and reflects on how the framework could be developed.

The paper is set out as follows. The first section establishes the importance and interest in studying clothes retailing, and the case of M&S, the largest UK clothes retailer. The second explains why business model theory and business case theory for sustainability can be used together to identify patterns of systemic change. The methodology is explained in the next section. The fourth section has the results, the fifth discusses them, and the final section provides a conclusion.

Retailers, clothing and innovation for sustainable consumption

Many researchers have sought to understand and explain how long-established systems of production and consumption could be influenced to transform through innovation, in order to achieve the goal of dramatically increased environmentally sustainability (Tukker et al., 2008; Shove, 2003; Berkhout *et al.*, 2004). Large existing businesses are seen as being trapped in systemic interdependencies (Tukker *et al.*, 2008). This is especially so in consumer businesses with short-term profit focus, such as retailers (Charter *et al.*, 2008). On one hand, individual firms are said to have too limited a role to make changes happen in systems (Smith *et al.*, 2005), yet, on the other, large businesses have a broad reach of influence (Hockerts and Wüstenhagen, 2010). This paper examines one large business in order to assess if and how its activities in the clothing system could represent system innovation for material scale improvement in environmental sustainability.

Systems of clothing in developed markets are large, complex and wide-ranging; in 2011, £41 billion was spent on clothing in the UK (Mintel, 2012b); it is the second largest consumer goods category after food and drink at £102 billion (Mintel, 2013). Spaargaren (2011) identifies clothing as one of the sectors in which socio-technical transitions approaches for increased sustainability have been least applied (in comparison with food and housing). The UK Government also identified clothing as one of ten priority areas for action for sustainable consumption and production (DEFRA, 2010b). It brought together nearly 300 clothing stakeholders (including businesses, charities and NGOs) to work on a Sustainable Clothing Action Plan (DEFRA, 2010a). The output included a schematic of the life cycle of clothing and its extensive environmental and social impacts (DEFRA, 2010b: 5). In clothes retailing and consumption, each of the stages has a complex socio-technical system of its own; in the use phase alone, Shove (2003: 137) describes a complex 'system of systems' just for domestic clothes laundering. Figure 1 shows six interrelated systems in the 'Use Chain'

Figure 1 **The Use Chain for clothing**
Source: developed by the author, informed by DEFRA (2010b) and Shove (2003).

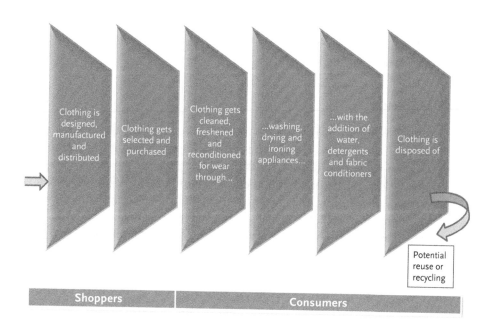

and the businesses that provide products and services within it. This has been built on the Sustainable Clothing Action Plan (DEFRA, 2010a), Shove (2003) and on Solomon and Rabolt's (2004) explanation of the interrelated systems in the retailing, consumption and disposal of clothing.

This Use Chain distinguishes between shoppers (or 'customers' in M&S reports) and consumers. The process of clothes shopping has become a leisure activity in its own right, over 50% of women agreeing that it fulfils a need for entertainment (Corker, 2011). The term 'consumer' is reserved for those wearing, cleaning, washing, drying, ironing and, later, recycling, or otherwise disposing of clothes. The cycle of use and re-use requires detergents, appliances, water, and power (Shove, 2003), before disposal, possible alteration, re-use or recycling.

In each of the Use Chain systems, retailers of clothing are intermediaries between shoppers and manufacturers, potentially playing a number of relevant roles for sustainable consumption. First, they proactively construct the shape and constraints for consumers' consumption choices, for instance in 'choice editing' (Charter et al., 2008). Second, they are gatekeepers for good consumption behaviour (Lee et al., 2012; Solomon and Rabolt, 2004) and, third, they represent their views of consumer needs to government (Marsden and Wrigley, 1995; DEFRA, 2010b). Therefore retailers are an influential link in the production and consumption chain for consumer goods such as clothes.

The demand for more frequent replacement of clothing has increased over recent years (O'Cass, 2004). More garments are being disposed of after being worn relatively few times (Birtwistle and Moore, 2007; McAfee et al., 2007). Reasons given for this include price decreases (Morgan and Birtwistle, 2009), due to clothing being sourced at lower cost from developing countries (Jones et al., 2005). Furthermore retailers have promoted 'fast fashion', thereby increasing the frequency of purchase of clothing to five or more 'seasons' (Solomon and Rabolt, 2004), through heightened trend exploitation, and supported by shorter development cycles (Reinach, 2005; Tokatli, 2008; Tokatli et al., 2008). This has led to an increasingly detrimental environmental impact (Ritch and Schröder, 2012).

Marks & Spencer

M&S is the long-term market leader in clothes retailing in the UK (Mintel, 2012b, 2012a, 2010, 2009, 2008, 2007), with a longstanding reputation for quality at good value (Worth, 2007). Its main categories of goods are clothing and food (Marks & Spencer, 2013a) and is predominantly a UK business; the UK accounts for 88% of its sales revenue, through 790 stores and online sales (Marks & Spencer, 2013c). The firm is long-established; it was registered as a limited company in 1903 (Worth, 2007). M&S sells clothing under its own registered brand names only and therefore is fully responsible for the supply chain and manufacture of the clothing it sells. From the 1930s M&S has invested in technological innovation in textiles in its supply chain; for instance, in the 1950s and 1960s the company led the mass market availability of clothing manufactured using new synthetic textiles (Worth, 2007). Fletcher (2008) reported that, more than ten years previously, M&S had been working to reduce the environmental impact of its clothing. M&S's specific competitive advantages in clothing arise from its trusted consumer reputation for quality (Worth, 2007), long-established capabilities in considering environmental impacts (Blowfield, 2013), and its textile design and sourcing expertise (Khan *et al.*, 2008). These enable M&S to impact the whole Use Chain for the environmental sustainability of the clothing system and to 'simultaneously exercise demand-power upwards and supply-power downwards' (Huber, 2008: 362).

M&S has a well-defined corporate responsibility programme, launched in January 2007 as 'Plan A' (Marks & Spencer, 2007), consisting of 100 individual initiatives in five areas. In 2010, the five areas were restructured, renumbered and extended, and a further 80 were added, making 180 in total. All the initiatives are tracked within the company's annual reports: 'How We Do Business' (Marks & Spencer, 2013b). In order to find patterns of systemic change arising from Plan A in clothing, this paper will next identify the relevant business model innovation literature.

Business models and innovation

The concept of the business model has become increasingly used to provide explanations and tools for studying the dynamics of businesses (Zott *et al.*, 2011), emerging as e-commerce firms were established and grew. These were often characterised by service that was free at the point of use. Therefore it was not always obvious how the provision of value to customers was to lead to economic value being generated for the business owners. Business model concepts showed how value could be created in these circumstances. Given this provenance, some concepts prioritise the creation of economic value for the business (Zott *et al.*, 2011; Chesbrough and Rosenbloom, 2002; Johnson *et al.*, 2008). A frequently used approach from Osterwalder and Pigneur (2010) deconstructs the business model into nine interrelated 'building blocks'. These blocks require specification of the value proposition (VP), the key resources, the key partnerships, the key activities, the customer segments, the customer relationships, the channels, the cost structure, and the revenue streams.

The concept of competitive advantage, the capacity to improve and innovate continuously (Porter and van der Linde, 1995), is treated by authors within business model analysis differently. Teece (2010) and Magretta (2002) explicitly exclude it and regard it as part of consideration of business strategy whereas Morris (2005), and Chesbrough and Rosenbloom (2002) include it. Johnson *et al.* (2008) regard competitive advantage as resulting from the unique way the elements of the business model are put together. Competitive advantage will also be considered later in connection with business cases for sustainability, since it seems important when considering system-level innovation.

The business case for sustainability

The business model concept has recently been employed in the context of sustainable innovation (Boons and Lüdeke-Freund, 2013; Wüstenhagen and Boehnke, 2008; Wells, 2008; Hannon *et al.*, 2013). Because it is used to define a company's activities in the context of its customers and the entities it interacts with, where those activities take place, and the resulting value accrued, by whom, it therefore enables the business to be seen as part of a system, rather than operating in isolation (Johnson and Suskewicz, 2009).

Schaltegger *et al.* (2012) condense Osterwalder and Pigneur's (2010) nine business model innovation 'building blocks' into four pillars (A, B, C and D in Figure 2). A high degree of business model innovation relates to changes that can be identified across all four pillars (Schaltegger *et al.*, 2012).

Figure 2 Business model innovation canvas, and business model pillars: nine building blocks shown in grey; four pillars, A, B, C and D, shown in black

Source: adapted from Osterwalder and Pigneur (2010) and Schaltegger *et al.* (2012).

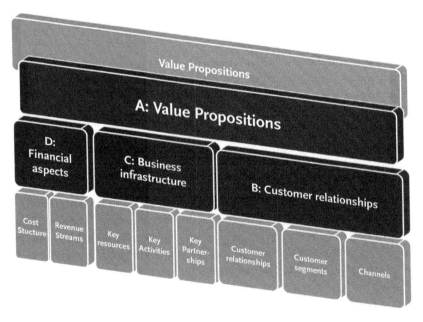

Schaltegger *et al.* (2012) use the four pillars of the business model from Figure 2 on one axis and use business case drivers for sustainability on the other, to show the interrelationships between them, as shown in Table 1. Business case drivers arise from the choices to be made in each business (Hahn *et al.*, 2010), appropriate to that business's strategy (Porter and Kramer, 2006). Researchers have categorised these choices in different ways across a number of business case drivers (Porter and Kramer, 2006; Garriga and Melé, 2004; Hoffman and Henn, 2008; Okereke, 2007; Bansal and Roth, 2000). Schaltegger et al.'s (2012) approach identifies business case drivers in six categories and cross-analyses them against observed elements of the business model. Once again, firm-specific competitive advantages are not explicitly included in this framework, yet strengthening and creating these through sustainability strategies has been regarded as important by a number of authors (Porter and Kramer, 2006; Kolk and Pinkse, 2008). However, this framework is used here because it uniquely combines the assessment of degrees of business model innovation with the ways in which the initiatives have addressed the core drivers of the business case.

Table 1 Framework showing interrelations between business model and business case drivers for sustainability

Source: simplified from Schaltegger et al. (2012)

Core drivers of business cases for sustainability	Generic business model pillars for new, more sustainable products or services			
	Pillar A Value Proposition (VP)	Pillar B Customer Relationships	Pillar C Business Infrastructure	Pillar D Financial Aspects
Costs and cost reduction	Lower costs for customers	Closed-loop service systems	Lower costs through partnerships	Balancing cost reductions for customers and the business's cost structure
Sales and profit margin	Environmental superiority generates sales and profits	Increased customer retention and value per customer	Partnerships deliver or overcome market barriers	New customer relationships contribute to diversified revenue streams
Risk and risk reduction	Lowering risks to society is valued by some customer segments	Reduced sustainability risks for customers lead to higher customer loyalty	Partnerships can minimise internal and external risks	Improved risk and credit rating resulting from lowered sustainability risks
Reputation and brand value	Good corporate reputation	Increased customer loyalty from marketing sustainability	Strategic partnerships enhance company reputation	Good ratings in sustainability indices

Continued

Core drivers of business cases for sustainability	Generic business model pillars for new, more sustainable products or services			
	Pillar A Value Proposition (VP)	Pillar B Customer Relationships	Pillar C Business Infrastructure	Pillar D Financial Aspects
Attractiveness as employer	Employees identify with VPs	Better customer service as a result of higher employee motivation	Partners encounter motivated employees	Increased employee retention leading to lower costs
Innovative capabilities	New VPs arise as sustainability potential is recognised	Innovative products and services improve customer retention	New activities and partnerships	Higher innovation potential leading to an increase of shareholder value

Methodology

In order to explore sustainable consumption within the Use Chain for clothing, a case study of a subset of M&S's Plan A's initiatives were chosen. The 100 original 2007 Plan A commitments were selected on the basis of two criteria:

▶ Those that apply, at least in part, to M&S's business in the clothing system

▶ Those that are designed directly to encourage consumers to behave more sustainably, for environmental benefit, in the use of clothing. Initiatives for reducing, recycling, and recyclability of packaging, plastic bags, and clothes hangers were excluded because these are related to shoppers, rather than consumers

Eight initiatives were selected and then reviewed by content analysis of three of the six annual 'How We Do Business' reports, together with the longer term review report 'The key lessons from the Plan A business case' (Marks & Spencer, 2012a). The first and last reports were chosen (Marks & Spencer, 2007, 2013b) so that what had been said to have been achieved over the maximum time period could be assessed. In 2010, Plan A as a whole was increased in scope and its aims restructured (Marks & Spencer, 2010), so this report was also selected for analysis, as the mid-point of the period. Key words were searched for, based on those that corresponded with the criteria in Schaltegger *et al.*'s framework. The key words used were 'cost/s', 'sales', 'profit', 'risk', 'reputation', 'brand', 'loyalty', 'employee', 'staff' (while not in the framework, this word seemed to be synonymous with 'employee' within the reports), 'innovation', 'innovative', and 'business model'. The relative quantities of word counts within the framework were used to assess the business case rationale and business model pillar according to the framework (see Table 3 in the Appendix).

M&S had no direct involvement in this research, but Oxfam, as an NGO partner with M&S for one of the initiatives, was contacted to understand the extent of the effect of one of the initiatives on their own business model. Written responses to questions were received. The outcomes and results of each initiative were then mapped onto the framework (Table 1), by selecting the business case drivers and business model pillars indicated by the terms used in the data, related to the specific initiatives. The actions set out within DEFRA's (2010b) Sustainable Clothing Action Plan were used to cross check the originality and distinctiveness of M&S's initiatives against its UK competitors, in order to assess the extent of firm-specific advantage that they represented .The completed framework was used to evaluate the degree of business model innovation, by assessing the number of business model elements that had changed. Finally the initiatives were mapped on the Use Chain to assess which of them impacted across more than one of the interrelated systems.

Results

Marks & Spencer Plan A commitments across the period

Table 2 shows the description of the aim of each of the eight initiatives and their status across the three selected years, together with the elements identified using the framework. Six of the eight initiatives selected were declared achieved by 2010 and the other two declared to be 'on plan' (Marks & Spencer, 2010). All eight nevertheless remain among the 180 initiatives reported in 2013 (Marks & Spencer) . The 2007 Plan A launch numbering is used as the principle reference throughout this paper (the 2010 numbering scheme is shown also in Table 2). Two of the eight (26 and 44) were restructured in 2010 to form two of the additional 80 created that year. It suggests that some of these initiatives were seen as experimental and ambitious; not all were achieved, but led to new targets later; a 'learning by doing' approach.

At the start in 2007, the specificity of the descriptions of the eight initiatives varies, ranging from clear, measurable, and timed targeting, to non-measurable intentions to support the work of others. Three of the initiatives that were declared achieved in 2010 were single stage activities having no element of outcome measurement (25, 27, 28, see Table 2). It is notable that each of the other commitments that remained current in 2010 had been rephrased to include both an outcome assessment standard and a specific date target. This indicates that the need to monitor and justify results over time led to reconstruction of the aims in a way that allowed for clear measurement of outcomes.

Table 2 The eight Plan A commitments selected for analysis, their status across three years, 2007, 2010, 2012, and summary of their business driver and business model impact using Schaltegger et al.'s (2012) framework (the full analysis is shown in the Appendix)

2007 no	Name of initiative	Aim description (Marks & Spencer, 2007)	Status (Marks & Spencer, 2010)	Status (Marks & Spencer, 2013b, 2012a)	Elements observed using Schaltegger et al. (2012) framework
44	Customer recycling services	Introducing a range of recycling services for our customers including a project for used clothing	Restructured into two commitments: 12.2 'Help our customers recycle 20 million items of clothing each year by 2015'; and 12.12, for which 'by 2012' was added to the original 2007 wording and it was declared achieved; the Oxfam Clothes Exchange was launched in 2008	12.2: declared to be 'On Plan', 3 million garments having been donated in the previous year, the fourth year of collaboration with Oxfam. The initiative was rebranded 'Shwopping' in April 2012 and further plans declared to buy recycled materials back from Oxfam as raw materials for new garments 12.12: No further update since 2010. Further development through a trial with Oxfam and the British Heart Foundation for recycling furniture	The value proposition and customer relationships were created through a closed-loop system that made it easy, convenient, and attractive for customers to recycle at M&S stores and rewarded them with a £5 voucher. More customers visited M&S on clothing return days. Customers were later able to buy a low cost wool coat that M&S had arranged through its suppliers to be made with recycled fibres M&S created new infrastructure and new partnerships to process the items that were returned or faulty, and to collect clothes through Oxfam stores. Oxfam has a pre-existing trading division to re-sell, reuse, and recycle clothes. 'Recycle at Oxfam' appears on clothing care labels. Both M&S and Oxfam had worked previously on the Sustainable Clothing Action plan M&S benefited financially because the recycled fibres in the wool coat reduced the raw material costs and, it is assumed, there were additional sales revenues from the increased customer visits Oxfam also benefited from the items brought to them, raising £2.6m to 2012, arising from the increased number of collection points and audience for, and awareness of, the service

| 26 | Low carbon products | Developing and selling products with a lower carbon impact | Changed to: 'Develop a low carbon products and services business, including the provision of energy and insulation services by 2010'. Became commitment 9.5 In addition, a new commitment was introduced: 9.3 'Energy Efficient Electrical Products'. Aim wording: 'Ensure that by 2015 at least 90% of our household electrical products meet a credible energy efficiency standard and improve the energy efficiency of the most energy intensive products by at least 25%' | 9.5 declared achieved; a new, separate business 'Marks & Spencer Energy' had been created in 2008, offering energy supply, solar panel installation and insulation services 9.3 declared to be 'On plan'. The products were said to have included washing machines and tumble dryers, but M&S no longer sold these from 31/08/2012 (Marks & Spencer, 2012c) | The new M&S energy business required new infrastructure, new partnerships, created a new revenue and profit source, arising from services M&S had not previously sold. It gave customers a new value proposition through cost incentives for reduced energy use and enabled cross selling and easy access to the service for existing customers. Employees benefited from free home insulation |

Continued

83

2007 no	Name of initiative	Aim description (Marks & Spencer, 2007)	Status (Marks & Spencer, 2010)	Status (Marks & Spencer, 2013b, 2012a)	Elements observed using Schaltegger et al. (2012) framework
27	Footprint campaign	Launching campaigns with the WWF and National Federation of Women's Institutes—to help our customers and employees understand their carbon footprint and how to reduce it	Became commitment 9.6 and declared achieved	No further update since 2010	WI members pledged to save around 10,000 tonnes of CO_2 through the campaign; implying it enhanced M&S's reputation with this group. Public link with NGOs (in the case of WWF, on their website) enhances their reputation
28	The Climate Group campaign	Working with the Climate Group on a major educational campaign in 2007 encouraging people to wash clothes at 30°C to cut energy use and CO_2 emissions	Became commitment 9.7 and declared achieved	No further update since 2010	The value proposition was originally communicated as designed to help customers cut CO_2 emissions (therefore to gain loyalty from marketing sustainability) but changed in 2009 to emphasise the cost reduction customers could achieve: 'Wash at 30°C save up to 40% energy' appears on many M&S clothing care labels

The Journal of Corporate Citizenship Issue 57 *March 2015*

| 55 | Cotton | Launching a sustainability strategy covering all our cotton including approaches such as 'Fairtrade', organic and the international cotton industry 'Better Cotton Initiative' by 2008

This commitment overlaps with initiative 81:
'Fairtrade' clothing: Converting 20 million clothing garments including £5 plain t-shirts, women's strappy vests, oxford shirts to 'Fairtrade' cotton—equal to 10% of all M&S cotton use' | Changed to 'Procure Sustainable Cotton', with the aim: 'Procure 25% of cotton from sustainable sources by 2015 and 50% by 2020'. This said now to include 'Fairtrade, organic, "Better Cotton Initiative", recycled fibres and other, more sustainable forms of cotton production' (2010:10).
(Now commitment 16.15)

Declared M&S had, in 2009, 'become the UK's largest retailer of Fairtrade certified cotton clothing' (2010: 12), nevertheless the initiative number 81 was declared to be 'Behind Plan' since Fairtrade certified cotton was estimated to have been 2.5% of all the cotton M&S used against the target of 10%
(Now commitment 17.20) | 16.15 declared to be 'On plan', having sold over 8 million items made from these materials, 3.8% of total cotton usage
17.20 declared 'Not achieved' due to the complexity and availability of Fairtrade cotton in the supply chain. It was estimated that 1% of cotton used was Fairtrade, representing a reduction from 2010
The commitment is to be replaced by the overall commitment, 16.15 | The activities under this commitment contributed to reducing future financial risk arising from shortage of cotton, a key raw material for M&S
The partnership with the 'Better Cotton Initiative' membership organisation had business infrastructure benefits, for instance, reduced risks and barriers compared to acting alone. However the Fairtrade partnership did not meet its objectives apparently due to supply chain difficulties |

Continued

2007 no	Name of initiative	Aim description (Marks & Spencer, 2007)	Status (Marks & Spencer, 2010)	Status (Marks & Spencer, 2013b, 2012a)	Elements observed using Schaltegger et al. (2012) framework
60	Polyester	Using recycled plastic (e.g. used bottles) to make polyester, rather than using oil. Make ranges of men's, women's and children's polyester fleeces from recycled plastic within a year. Extend to other polyester ranges such as trousers, suits, and furniture 'fill' by 2012	Became commitment 16.20 and declared achieved	Declared to have been 'Previously achieved'. The 2011 report (Marks & Spencer, 2011) had noted that the use of recycled polyester increased from 1100 tonnes to 1900 tonnes from 2010 to 2011	The use of recycled polyester rather than new polyester, derived from oil, is well established and is not unique to M&S

54	Sustainable textiles	Reducing the environmental impact of the textiles we sell by trialling new fibres such as bamboo, renewable plastics, and new ways of producing fibres such as organic cotton, linen, and wool	Changed to: 'Reducing the environmental impact of the textiles we sell throughout our supply chain by 2012'. Became commitment 16.14 and declared achieved	No further update since 2010	The originally worded commitment indicated a desire to mitigate the business infrastructure risk of future raw material supply issues. The later wording implied innovative supply infrastructure actions and therefore no longer sought to influence consumption directly
25	Carbon labelling	Supporting The Carbon Trust to develop a carbon-labelling scheme for consumer products	Became commitment 9.4 and declared achieved. M&S chose not to adopt the carbon-labelling scheme	No further update since 2010	None, as no action was taken as a result of this commitment

Selected Plan A commitments in relation to business model pillars, competitive advantages and business case drivers

Seven of the eight initiatives were mapped on Schaltegger *et al.*'s (2012) framework for cross analysis, summarised in Table 2 and shown in detail in Table 3 (see Appendix). The eighth, the development of a Carbon labelling scheme (25), was not implemented and therefore was not mapped. Looking at the pattern of the business drivers, it is costs, sales revenue, and reputation that are most prominent. Plan A as a whole was originally planned to cost £40m per year, but became cost neutral in its second, and had delivered net business benefits of £105m in total up to 2012 (Marks & Spencer, 2012a). Therefore the business case has been secured through cost savings.

As for risk, there is substantial evidence of M&S working with NGO and government partners such as Oxfam (44), DEFRA (54), WWF (27 and 55), The Climate Group (28), and The Carbon Trust (25), although not explicitly for risk mitigation. Innovation capability appears as a justification only in the more recent reports. The publicly declared five-year time horizon is said to have enabled M&S to implement more far-reaching change than would otherwise be possible on a usual shareholder-led one year planning timetable. Attractiveness as an employer did not feature strongly for these initiatives, not surprisingly, since they were selected for analysis based on design for consumer impact. Yet internal structure and personal incentives changed over the period to enable the business to become more integrated and responsive in its management of Plan A and this may have had an effect on employee motivation.

Thinking of M&S's firm-specific competitive advantages, four of the initiatives relied on, and may have strengthened, M&S's capacity to innovate through textile design and sourcing (44, 54, 55 and 60). Three (26, 27, 28) capitalise on M&S's trusted customer reputation. Its environmental impact expertise underpins four of the initiatives (25, 28, 54, 55).

At a broader level, the extent of business model innovation can now be identified. Two of the commitments feature in all four columns, indicating that they each represent a high degree of business model innovation: low carbon products (26) and clothes recycling in partnership with Oxfam (44). The first of these led to a new business for M&S: energy supply and insulation services. However, there is no evidence that new business models were intended to result from Plan A at its start (Marks & Spencer, 2007). In the latest report, there is explicit reference to the need for new business models (Marks & Spencer, 2013b). Therefore incremental achievements seem to have led to the creation of new business models, rather than new business models being planned initially.

Selected Plan A commitments in relation to the Use Chain

Three of the initiatives act across the Use Chain (Figure 3). First, processing of discarded clothing (44) produced recycled fibres to be used in new garments. M&S organised partnerships with Oxfam, its textile suppliers, and processors so that recycled textiles could be reintroduced as material for new garments. M&S report increased numbers of shoppers on clothing return days (Marks & Spencer, 2012a) and give a £5 voucher redeemable against a future purchase to those returning clothes. M&S communicated this initiative to consumers as 'every time you buy something new, give us something old' (Marks & Spencer, 2012b), positioning the trigger for action as the purchase of a new item, rather than the trigger being the receipt of a voucher. Nevertheless, it is reasonable to assume that some of the £5 vouchers led to new sales of clothing items. If these sales represent additional sales in the market (rather than substitution of sales that would have occurred in other retailers) then the initiative has resulted in a rebound effect of greater consumption, rather than less. However it has also created a new closed-loop mechanism and new consumer recycling actions, through easy, risk-free, and cost-free mechanisms for customers.

Second, M&S promoted lower temperature washing. Other retail businesses such as Asda, Sainsbury, and Tesco (DEFRA, 2010b), detergent manufacturers (Unilever, 2012; Business in the Community, 2008) and appliance manufacturers (AMDEA, 2013) have done the same. However M&S's initiative to wash at 30° appears to present a future opportunity, shown by the 'bubble' box in Figure 3, to partner with companies selling more energy efficient washing machines and detergents, by proactively making clothing available that is designed to be washed at low temperatures. Third, they created a new business to sell energy services.

Figure 3 The Use Chain for clothing showing Plan A commitments that extend across systems

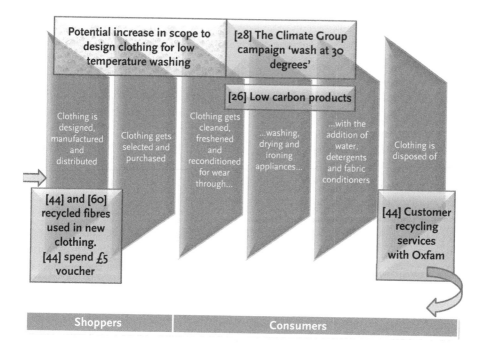

Discussion

System innovation

None of M&S's clothing commitments exhibits fourfold or tenfold systemic improvement in environmental efficiency. Yet perhaps clothing recycling could represent the 'take off' phase towards a system innovation (Kemp, 2008: 371), since the commitment originally was to provide a service for customers to recycle their clothes, but this became a new recycle loop, even though this had not been planned at the start. Furthermore, M&S worked with Oxfam and its raw material suppliers as partners, to design and encourage new consumer practice, to lead and create a new market (for clothes using the recycled material), and devise a new infrastructure of service and provision. This analysis has shown examples of positive outcomes from 'learning by doing' within an established large consumer business.

M&S's commitment over a long period, and adjustments that it has made to its own organisation to facilitate the further development of Plan A, show that an established business can develop new business models in the interest of achieving long-term sustainability goals. While many reasons have been given for regime actors not seeking system change (Elzen *et al.*, 2004), there is evidence here that M&S have not felt entirely constrained by these. In this case, business model innovation took place as a result of initiatives being taken and developed over the years, not as an explicitly declared intention at the start.

The use of the analytical framework

Three points can be drawn from the use of Schaltegger *et al.*'s (2012) framework. First, it proved useful for categorising the elements of the initiatives across both business case drivers and business model pillars. This enabled two new business models to be identified by looking across the pillars, yet M&S's core clothes retailing business model has remained its main sales and profit driver. It is not that this business model has been redesigned, but added to. This suggests that further theoretical approaches would be of value, to conceptualise degrees of business model innovation.

Second, by identifying where M&S has used its established firm-specific competitive advantages, this paper has also identified difficulties for other retailers who may seek to follow their approach. However, the framework lacks a way to recognise existing competitive advantages on which innovative capability can be built further. Third, an limitation of the use of this framework for only some of the initiatives in 'Plan A', is that the individual initiatives are merely part of the whole Plan A picture, to which business case drivers might be attributed by M&S within the reports, rather than to individual initiatives.

Separately, the novel Use Chain framework has identified activities and further opportunities across a number of interrelated systems in clothing. It has highlighted new opportunities for clothing businesses to work in partnership with other businesses across the chain to reduce consumption emissions. It serves also to emphasise the critical role of retailers within and across each of these systems; this has not previously been identified in this way.

Conclusion

This paper acknowledges the leadership shown by M&S and its capability in moulding its sustainability initiatives over time, through learning from its results, within a strong, transparent and coherent framework. M&S itself does not believe that unit volume consumption will decline, yet it declares that it will continue to seek closed-loop and service-based solutions for the future (Marks & Spencer, 2012a). As the market leader in the UK, the firm has undertaken ambitious environmental goals and built new business models. This is contrary to the predictions of many researchers. It has not been wholly trapped in a system, as Tukker *et al.* (2008) describe it, but has found ways to start to change within a system, by taking a long-term perspective and seeking to influence consumer behaviour.

While M&S has seen business case benefits from the strategic choices it has made through Plan A, as Porter and Kramer (2006) predict for individual businesses, M&S's competitive advantages make it less valuable for competitors to imitate the initiatives, serving as barriers to those competitors participating in system change. For wider system change, it would be beneficial if these barriers could be overcome. Therefore perhaps the role of government is to recognise when businesses have created a new business model for a more sustainable consumption system and subsequently to support the system's continuing development through finding ways to make it attractive for other businesses to take part.

Appendix

Table 3 Mapping seven selected initiatives from Marks & Spencer Plan A (Marks & Spencer, 2007, 2010, 2013b, 2012a) on Schaltegger *et al.*'s (2012) framework

Core drivers of business cases for sustainability	Generic business model pillars			
	Value proposition	Customer relationships	Business infrastructure	Financial aspects
Costs and cost reduction	Lower energy costs for consumers (26 and 28). The 'Wash at 30°' campaign was repositioned in 2009 to emphasise the money saving opportunity rather than the CO_2 emissions saving	Clothes recycling enabled customers to get £5 voucher redeemable against a future purchase of over £35 and enabled M&S to sell a low cost wool coat (44)	Waste wool from donated and faulty garments reprocessed within the supply chain (44)	Use of recycled wool in a new design of women's coat enabled cost reduction in raw materials (44)
Sales and profit margin	Increase sales encouraged by voucher redemption having recycled clothes via M&S stores and Oxfam (44)	M&S benefited from increased numbers of customers on clothing return days (44)	Low carbon products, services for energy supply, other services through M&S Energy, a new business set up in October 2008 in partnership with Scottish and Southern Energy (26)	Cross selling the new M&S Energy service generated new profits and diversified M&S's revenue stream (26) New sales revenue from additional customer visits on clothing return days (44)
Risk and risk reduction		Risk-free recycling	M&S predict raw material supply issues under climate change therefore Plan A helps to ensure future raw material supplies (54) (55)	

Reputation brand value	Being seen to encourage recycling of clothes through the Shwopping initiative (44) Being seen to reward consumers for their household energy reduction (26) Footprint campaign (27)	Footprint campaign (27) The Climate Group campaign to wash at 30° (28)	Footprint campaign (WWF and WI) (27). Increased visibility for Plan A through network of Oxfam stores (44) and for WWF through the linked website (WWF, 2013) (27) Further communication benefits for Oxfam on clothing care labels (60) and £2.6m raised for Oxfam from the scheme from launch to 2012 Contribution to DEFRA's Sustainable Clothing Action Plan (54) Use of recycled polyester from bottles instead of oil, for polyester garments and fill (60)
Attractiveness as employer			Footprint campaign (27) and free home insulation (26) for employees both enhance the effectiveness of Plan A itself

Continued

Core drivers of business cases for sustainability	Generic business model pillars			
	Value proposition	Customer relationships	Business infrastructure	Financial aspects
Innovative capabilities	The initial Clothing Exchange days with Oxfam were innovative (44) The second phase of clothes recycling has led M&S to create a social network for like-minded customers (44)	1. New service for customers (44) (convenient to take clothes back to Oxfam) 2. £5 M&S vouchers from energy and energy-related services increase customer retention (26)	The Oxfam partnership served to simplify the logistics for M&S in taking clothes back (44) while increasing the service access points for customers New partnership with WWF (27) (55) and with Scottish and Southern Electricity (26) Closed loop system for wool and cashmere when included in new garments (44) Trialling new textile fibres (54)	M&S Energy was set up as a separate financial entity (26)

Note. Numbering shown in brackets refers to the 2007 report (Marks & Spencer, 2007)

References

Allwood, C., Laursen, S., Derodriguez, C. & Bocken, N. 2006. Well Dressed? The Present and Future Sustainability of Clothing and Textiles in the United Kingdom, University of Cambridge. *Institute for Manufacturing, Cambridge.*

Amdea. 2013. *Time To Change* [Online]. Available: http://www.t2c.org.uk/washing/energy-saving-tips/.

Bansal, P. & Roth, K. 2000. Why Companies Go Green: A Model of Ecological Responsiveness *The Academy of Management Journal*, 43, 717-736.

Berkhout, F., Smith, A. & Stirling, A. 2004. Socio-technical regimes and transitions contexts. *In:* Elzen, B., Geels, F. W. & Green, K. (eds.) *System Innovation and the Transition to Sustainability.* Cheltenham: Edward Elgar.

Birtwistle, G. & Moore, C. 2007. Fashion clothing: where does it all end up? *International Journal of Retail & Distribution Management*, 35, 210-216.

Blowfield, M. 2013. *Business and Sustainability*, Oxford University Press.

Boons, F. & Lüdeke-Freund, F. 2013. Business models for sustainable innovation: State-of-the-art and steps towards a research agenda. *Journal of Cleaner Production*, 45, 9-19.

BUSINESS IN THE COMMUNITY. 2008. *Procter & Gamble - Ariel Turn to 30* [Online]. Available: http://www.bitc.org.uk/resources/case_studies/pg_rm.html [Accessed April 17th 2012].

Charter, M., Gray, C., Clark, T. & Woolman, T. 2008. Review: The role of business in realising sustainable consumption and production. *System Innovation for Sustainability: Perspectives on Radical Changes to Sustainable Consumption and Production*, 46-69.

Chesbrough, H. W. & Rosenbloom, R. S. 2002. The role of the business model in capturing value from innovation: Evidence from Xerox Corporation's technology spinoff companies. *Industrial and Corporate Change*, 11, 533-534.

Corker, H. 2011. Fashion Forward: UK Trends in Clothes Shopping. London: The Future Foundation.

Defra. 2010a. *Product Road Maps: Clothing* [Online]. Available: http://archive.defra.gov.uk/environment/business/products/roadmaps/clothing/index.htm [Accessed March 21st 2013].

Defra. 2010b. Sustainable Clothing Action Plan. Available: http://www.defra.gov.uk/publications/2011/03/30/pb13206-clothing-action-plan/.

Elzen, B., Geels, F. W. & Green, K. 2004. *System innovation and the transition to sustainability: theory, evidence and policy*, Edward Elgar Publishing.

Fletcher, K. 2008. *Sustainable fashion and textiles: design journeys*, Earthscan.

Garriga, E. & Melé, D. 2004. Corporate Social Responsibility Theories: Mapping the Territory. *Journal of Business Ethics*, 53, 51-71.

Hahn, T., Figge, F. & Pinkse, J. 2010. Trade-offs in corporate sustainability: you can't have your cake and eat it. *Business Strategy and the Environment*, 19, 217-229.

Hannon, M. J., Foxon, T. J. & Gale, W. F. 2013. The co-evolutionary relationship between Energy Service Companies and the UK energy system: Implications for a low-carbon transition. *Energy Policy*.

Hockerts, K. & Wüstenhagen, R. 2010. Greening Goliaths versus emerging Davids: Theorizing about the role of incumbents and new entrants in sustainable entrepreneurship. *Journal of Business Venturing*, 25, 481-492.

Hoffman, A. J. & Henn, R. 2008. Overcoming the Social and Psychological Barriers to Green Building. *Organisation and Environment*, 21, 390-419.

Huber, J. 2008. Pioneer countries and the global diffusion of environmental innovations: Theses from the viewpoint of ecological modernisation theory *Global Environmental Change*, 18, 360-367.

Jackson, T. 2005. Motivating Sustainable Consumption: a review of evidence on consumer behaviour and behavioural change. London: Policy Studies Institute.

Jackson, T. (ed.) 2006. *The Earthscan reader in sustainable consumption*, London: Earthscan.

Johnson, M. W., Christensen, C. C. & Kagermann, H. 2008. Reinventing your business model. *Harvard Business Review*, 86, 50-59.

Jones, P., Hillier, D., Comfort, D. & Eastwood, I. 2005. Sustainable retailing and consumerism. *Management Research News*, 28, 34-44.

Kemp, R. 2008. Transition management for sustainable consumption and production. *In:* Tukker, A., Charter, M., Vezzoli, C., Stø, E. & Andersen, M. (eds.) *System Innovation for Sustainability.* Sheffield: Greenleaf.

Khan, O., Christopher, M. & Burnes, B. 2008. The impact of product design on supply chain risk: a case study. *International Journal of Physical Distribution & Logistics Management*, 38, 412-432.

Kolk, A. & Pinkse, J. 2008. A Perspective on Multinational Enterprises and Climate Change: Learning from 'An Inconvenient Truth'? *Journal of International Business Studies*, 39, 1359-1378.

Kozlowski, A., Bardecki, M. & Searcy, C. 2012. Environmental Impacts in the Fashion Industry. *Journal of Corporate Citizenship*, 2012, 16-36.

Lee, N., Choi, Y. J., Youn, C. & Lee, Y. 2012. Does Green Fashion Retailing Make Consumers More Eco-friendly? The Influence of Green Fashion Products and Campaigns on Green Consciousness and Behavior. *Clothing and Textiles Research Journal*, 30, 67-82.

Madsen, J., Hartlin, B., Perumalpillai, S., Selby, S. & Aumônier, S. 2007. Mapping of Evidence on Sustainable Development Impacts that Occur in Life Cycles of Clothing. Report to the Department for Environment, Food and Rural Affairs by Environmental Resources Management (ERM) Ltd. London: Defra.

Magretta, J. 2002. Why business models matter. *Harvard Business Review*, 80, 86-92.

Marks and Spencer. 2007. *How We Do Business* [Online]. Available: http://corporate.marksandspencer.com/howwedobusiness/hwdb_reports.

Marks and Spencer. 2010. *How We Do Business* [Online]. Available: http://corporate.marksandspencer.com/howwedobusiness/hwdb_reports.

Marks and Spencer. 2011. *How We Do Business* [Online]. Available: http://corporate.marksandspencer.com/howwedobusiness/hwdb_reports.

Marks and Spencer. 2012a. *The Key Lessons from the Plan A business case* [Online]. London: Marks & Spencer. Available: corporate.marksandspencer.com/documents/.../plan_a_report_2012.p...

Marks and Spencer. 2012b. *Shwopping Advert with Joanna Lumley* [Online]. Available: http://asustainablebusiness.com/ms-shwopping-advert-with-joanna-lumley-marks-and-spencer-2012/.

Marks and Spencer. 2012c. *Why can I not find domestic appliances online?* [Online]. Available: http://help.marksandspencer.com/faqs/ordering/domestic-appliances [Accessed March 24th 2013].

Marks and Spencer. 2013a. *Company Overview* [Online]. Available: http://corporate.marksandspencer.com/aboutus/company_overview [Accessed April 3rd 2013].

Marks and Spencer. 2013b. *How We Do Business reports* [Online]. Available: http://corporate.marksandspencer.com/howwedobusiness/hwdb_reports [Accessed January 13th 2014].

Marks and Spencer. 2013c. *Where we are* [Online]. Available: http://corporate.marksandspencer.com/aboutus/where/uk_stores [Accessed 23rd March 2013].

Marsden, T. & Wrigley, N. 1995. Regulation, retailing, and consumption. *Environment and Planning A*, 27, 1899-1912.

Mcafee, A., Dessain, V. & Sjöman, A. 2007. *Zara: IT for fast fashion*, Cambridge, Harvard Business School.

Mintel. 2007. *Clothing Retailing - UK* [Online]. Available: http://academic.mintel.com/sinatra/oxygen_academic/my_reports.

Mintel. 2008. *Clothing Retailing - UK* [Online]. Available: http://academic.mintel.com/sinatra/oxygen_academic/my_reports.

Mintel. 2009. *Clothing Retailing - UK* [Online]. Available: http://academic.mintel.com/sinatra/oxygen_academic/my_reports.

Mintel. 2010. *Clothing Retailing - UK* [Online]. Available: http://academic.mintel.com/sinatra/oxygen_academic/my_reports.

Mintel. 2012a. *Clothing Retailing - UK* [Online]. Available: http://academic.mintel.com/sinatra/oxygen_academic/my_reports.

Mintel. 2012b. *UK Washers and Dryers* [Online]. Available: http://academic.mintel.com/sinatra/oxygen_academic/my_reports.

Mintel 2013. Food and Drink Retailing.

Morgan, L. R. & Birtwistle, G. 2009. An investigation of young fashion consumers' disposal habits. *International journal of consumer studies*, 33, 190-198.

Morris, M., Schindehutte, M. & Allen, J. 2005. The entrepreneur's business model: Toward a unified perspective. *Journal of Business Research*, 58, 726-35.

O'Cass, A. 2004. Fashion clothing consumption: antecedents and consequences of fashion clothing involvement. *European Journal of Marketing*, 38, 869-882.

Okereke, C. 2007. An exploration of motivations, drivers and barriers to carbon management: The UK FTSE 100. *European Management Journal*, 25, 475-486.

Osterwalder, A. & Pigneur, Y. 2010. *Business Model Generation: A handbook for visionaries, game changers, and challengers*, John Wiley.

Porter, M. & van der Linde, C. 1995. Toward a New Conception of the Environment-Competitiveness Relationship. *The Journal of Economic Perspectives*, 9.

Porter, M. E. & Kramer, M. R. 2006. Strategy & Society: The Link Between Competitive Advantage and Corporate Social Responsibility. *Harvard Business Review*, 84, 78-92.

Reinach, S. S. 2005. China and Italy: fast fashion versus Pret a Porter. Towards a new culture of fashion. *Fashion Theory: The Journal of Dress, Body & Culture*, 9, 43-56.

Ritch, E. L. & Schröder, M. J. 2012. Accessing and affording sustainability: the experience of fashion consumption within young families. *International journal of consumer studies*, 36, 203-210.

Schaltegger, S., Lüdeke-Freund, F. & Hansen, E. G. 2012. Business cases for sustainability: the role of business model innovation for corporate sustainability. *International Journal of Innovation and Sustainable Development*, 6, 95-119.

Shove, E. 2003. *Comfort, cleanliness and convenience: the social organization of normality*, Oxford, Berg.

Smith, A., Stirling, A. & Berkhout, F. 2005. The governance of sustainable socio-technical transitions. *Research Policy*, 34, 1491-1510.

Solomon, M. & Rabolt, N. 2004. Consumer behavior in fashion. Englewood Cliffs, NJ: Prentice Hall.

Spaargaren, G. 2011. Theories of practices: Agency, technology, and culture: Exploring the relevance of practice theories for the governance of sustainable consumption practices in the new world-order. *Global Environmental Change*, 21, 813-822.

Teece, D. J. 2010. Business models, business strategy and innovation. *Long range planning*, 43, 172-194.

Tokatli, N. 2008. Global sourcing: insights from the global clothing industry—the case of Zara, a fast fashion retailer. *Journal of Economic Geography*, 8, 21-38.

Tokatli, N., Wrigley, N. & Kizilgün, Ö. 2008. Shifting global supply networks and fast fashion: made in Turkey for Marks & Spencer. *Global Networks*, 8, 261-280.

Tukker, A., Charter, M., Vezzoli, C., Sto, E. & Andersen, M. M. (eds.) 2008. *System innovation for sustainability: Perspectives on radical change to sustainable consumption and production*, Sheffield: Greenleaf.

Unilever. 2012. *Wash at 30°C* [Online]. Available: http://www.unilever.com/brands/hygiene andwelbeing/aroundthehouse/wash-at-30-degrees.aspx [Accessed April 17th 2012].

von Weizsäcker, E. U., Weizsäcker, E. U., Lovins, A. B. & Lovins, L. H. 1998. *Factor four: doubling wealth-halving resource use: the new report to the Club of Rome*, Earthscan Publications.

Wackernagel, M., Onisto, L. & Bello, P. A. 1997. *Ecological footprints of nations*, Universidad Anahuac de Xalapa, Centro de Estudios para la Sustentabilidad.

Wells, P. 2008. Alternative business models for a sustainable automotive industry. *In:* Tukker, A., Charter, M., Vezzoli, C., Stø, E. & Andersen, M. (eds.) *System Innovation for Sustainability.* Sheffield: Greenleaf.

Worth, R. 2007. *Fashion for the People: A History of Clothing at Marks & Spencer*, Berg Publishers.

Wüstenhagen, R. & Boehnke, J. 2008. Business models for sustainable energy. *In:* Tukker, A., Charter, M., Vezzoli, C., Stø, E. & Andersen, M. (eds.) *System Innovation for Sustainability.* Sheffield: Greenleaf.

WWF 2013. *Footprint Calculator* [Online]. Available: http://ms.footprint.wwf.org.uk/ [Accessed March 10th 2013].

Zott, C., Amit, R. & Massa, L. 2011. The business model: Recent developments and future research. *Journal of management,* 37, 1019-1042.

DOI: [10.9774/GLEAF.5001.2015.ma.00007]

Barriers towards a systemic change in the clothing industry

How do sustainable fashion enterprises influence their sector?

Ingrid Molderez and Bart Van Elst

University of Leuven, Belgium

This paper challenges one of the vital building blocks in the business model canvas, i.e. the 'key resources' that fashion enterprises need to be able to create value. Incumbent enterprises in the fashion industry tend to become more sustainable. In this movement towards sustainability, an important factor is the influence of pioneers in sustainable entrepreneurship. These pioneers are enterprises that have introduced sustainability in a way the market has not seen before. The text is inspired by Hockerts and Wüstenhagen (2010). They discuss the influence of small, sustainable start-ups on market incumbents; a process of co-evolution is emphasised. Hockerts and Wüstenhagen's model is a theoretical framework not yet tested by case studies in the fashion industry, which is the goal of this paper. The five enterprises selected for this research are characterised by a strong engagement towards sustainability: Stanley & Stella, ProGarments, Orimpex, Mayerline, and Van de Velde. These sustainable fashion enterprises play an important role because of their leadership and precedent role in sustainable innovation. The focus of the paper is on the act of 'influencing' in the fashion industry. Fashion companies need to be innovative in a sustainable way. Sharing this novelty to make the entire fashion industry more sustainable is difficult and, therefore, a barrier towards a systemic change in the clothing industry.

- Sustainable enterprises
- Innovation
- Influence
- Fashion industry

Ingrid Molderez is lecturer in corporate social responsibility and economics at KULeuven and researcher at CEDON, Centre for Economics and Corporate Sustainability. Ingrid's research is focused on sustainable entrepreneurship, sustainable innovation and other ways of thinking about sustainability, thereby drawing on ideas and images from many sources such as art, language, literature, apart from organisation theory, economics, social theory, and philosophy. Ingrid has a PhD in Applied Economic Sciences from University of Hasselt and a Master of Arts in Social Theory and Organisation from Keele University.

Faculty of Economics and Business, KU Leuven – University of Leuven, Campus Brussels, Warmoesberg 26, 1000 Brussels, Belgium

ingrid.molderez@kuleuven.be

Bart van Elst has a Bachelor Degree in International Marketing, a Master's Degree in Business Science and a Master's Degree in Applied Economic Sciences from Leuven University. He is freelance researcher with an interest in sustainable entrepreneurship. He runs his own enterprise in real estate.

Faculty of Economics and Business, KU Leuven – University of Leuven, Campus Brussels, Warmoesberg 26, 1000 Brussels, Belgium

van.elst.b@gmail.com

FASHION IS OMNIPRESENT IN MODERN society (Kawamura, 2006; Soeteman, 2010) and the fashion industry is subject to rapid changes of trends (Department for Environment, Food and Rural Affairs, 2010). This rapid change of trends means that the fashion industry is flexible, and, therefore, one could expect that the ideas of sustainability can more easily impregnate the fashion industry compared with a more stable sector. However, the same rapid change of trends also makes the fashion industry highly competitive. This competition leads to a historically unprecedented situation when apparel is priced far too low to reflect its true economic and ecological costs (Juliet, 2005), i.e. sustainability is sacrificed in favour of economic profit. A competitive price is ruling the game thereby outweighing people and planet. Over the last decades, there has been a strong upcoming move towards sustainability (Joergens, 2006; Lubin & Esty, 2010). In this movement, an important factor is the influence of enterprises strongly engaged in sustainability. This paper analyses whether and how these enterprises influence other enterprises or are being influenced by competitors in the fashion industry to become more sustainable.

To understand the nature of influence in business we start with a literature review. Despite the growing body of literature on sustainable fashion (Laitala & Boks, 2012), the area of inter-enterprise influence still remains uncharted. Therefore, we have conducted a series of interviews with representatives of five Belgian and Dutch fashion enterprises involved in sustainability: Stanley & Stella, Orimpex Organic Textiles, ProGarments, Mayerline, and Van de Velde. We have seen that enterprises active in sustainable fashion position themselves as an influencer for the fashion sector. However, it seems difficult for these enterprises to position themselves as an influenced enterprise. Being influenced carries a negative connotation of being a weak player in the sustainable fashion market.

Sustainable entrepreneurship

Pollution, depletion of resources, and the exploitation of workers have put pressure on companies to achieve more value for stakeholders other than shareholders (Esty et al., 2011). Stakeholders expect companies to contribute to sustainability issues that are relevant to their core business and where they can have the most impact (Du et al., 2010). This trend is further intensified by a growing concern of both the government and the public about climate change (Norberg-Bohm, 2010), quality of the groundwater (Vennemo et al., 2009), industrial pollution, food safety (Huanga et al., 2006), natural resource depletion (Weilenmann et al., 2010), and, especially in the fashion industry, abuse of workers (Hale & Shaw, 2002).

According to Cohen & Winn (2007) environmental quality declines due to inefficiency, externalities, flawed pricing mechanisms, and asymmetric information flows. However, these defects can also be viewed as an opportunity to develop new strategies in order to do business in a more sustainable way. Increasing interest in sustainability means that every self-respecting enterprise tries to profile itself as being sustainable (Crals & Vereeck, 2005). The transformation towards sustainability, however, is a continuum; there is no one-solution-fits-all concept because the more ambitious the corporate sustainability, the more complex the institutional structure (Van Marrewijk & Werre, 2003). The ISO 26000 standard guides a company towards corporate social responsibility (ISO, 2010).

The intended objective of a sustainable policy is to responsibly deal with environment and society. There are multiple reasons for companies to choose sustainability. Swanson (2008, p. 229) distinguishes between negative and positive motivations, 'negative when decision-makers act out of fear of adverse legal ramifications or pending legislation and positive when they voluntarily and affirmatively enact caring attitudes regarding their obligations to society'. She further stresses the pivotal role of moral leadership in implementing sustainability within an enterprise (Swanson, 2008, p. 231). Indeed, often the role of an ethics-inspired leader is of utmost importance (Goodpaster, 2004, 2007), as she or he lays the basis for the implementation of sustainability within the enterprise (Taubitz, 2010). Market innovations that drive sustainable development do not occur by accident; they have to be created by leaders who put them into the core of their business activities (Schaltegger, 2002). Integration of sustainability throughout the organisation is important to prevent a situation in which the sustainable policy gets lost with the departure of the leader (De Prins et al., 2009).

Implementation of sustainability, however, does not take place in a vacuum: managers are subject to a multitude of influences both internal and external (Swanson, 2008, p. 242). Influence is frequently used in scientific papers (Dworkin, 2003; Atuahene-Gima & De Luca, 2008; Jussim & Osgood, 1989), although not often in literature related to sustainability. Therefore, we frame this concept by looking at other sources not specialised in sustainability. In the context of social psychology, influence is defined as, 'one person causing changes (or preventing changes that would have occurred otherwise) in the attitudes (beliefs, behavior, etc.) of another' (Jussim & Osgood, 1989). Influence is defined as the extent to which an influence source is able to change the behaviours, opinions, and attitudes of an influence target (Atuahene-Gima & De Luca, 2008). Applying this definition to sustainability, we define influence as *an enterprise causing changes in products or production processes of other companies with the aim of sustainable transformations.*

One model which is particularly relevant in the context of sustainable transformations is that of Hockerts and Wüstenhagen (2010). Among different companies active in sustainability, they focus on two groups, 'Davids' and 'Goliaths'. 'Davids' are rather new and small enterprises with social and/or environmental objectives being at least as important as economic objectives; as opposed to 'Goliaths', which are old, incumbent, and large. Their economic objectives dominate while social/environmental objectives are complementary. As indicated by Hockerts and Wüstenhagen (2010), maturity processes can lead to some Davids becoming Goliaths or to Goliaths 'greening' their operations. Due to growing competition from the emerging Davids, incumbents engage in their own form of sustainable entrepreneurship. Often the players that are driven by a desire to achieve environmental and social change never grow beyond a small niche and, therefore, do not affect disruptive change. In a few cases, these can turn into sustainable entrepreneurs (Schaltegger, 2002) and alter the mass market. They are usually followed quite quickly by some market incumbents once early growth picks up. Later on, high-growth Davids orchestrate product innovation of the early Davids with the process innovation that Goliaths are good at. In a last stage sustainable entrepreneurs tend to extend to the mass-market brands, which begin to see a growing competitive threat from the start-ups and a market potential for themselves. Sustainable transformation of industries is however not going to be brought about by either Davids or Goliaths alone, but through their interaction. It is a co-evolution.

The influence that sustainable fashion enterprises have on companies in their sector is not adequately covered in the existing literature. The theoretical model of Hockerts and Wüstenhagen (2010) is therefore appropriate to analyse the existence of influence and co-evolution in the fashion industry.

Methodology

This paper takes a closer look at how sustainable fashion enterprises influence other players in the sector. We focus on companies in the fashion industry who have a strong record in relation to sustainability. We want to understand whether and how these fashion companies influence other companies in the sector. The selected companies are start-ups who have chosen to operate from a sustainable niche from the very beginning and incumbents who have an integrated sustainability strategy in their overall business.

In order to be able to answer the research question we will explore how the interviewees of the selected fashion enterprises think about the importance of 'influencing' the fashion sector towards sustainability and whether there is a common pattern of strategies among the different enterprises. An appropriate way to investigate these fashion enterprises is by means of case studies because we are interested in how and why questions (Yin, 1981). The selection of cases is based on purposed choice rather than at random since we want to focus on enterprises implementing strong sustainability policies within their daily organisational strategy.

We made use of information provided by professional associations each representing a number of textile enterprises such as Euratex; Fédération Belge de l'Industrie Textile, du Bois et de l'Ameublement (FEDUSTRIA); Creamoda; International Association of Users of Artificial and Synthetic Filament Yarns and of Natural Silk (IAUFFASS); European Man-made Fibers Association (CIRFS); European Association for Textile Polyolefins (EATP); International Association Serving the Nonwovens & Related Industries (EDANA); European Federation of the Cotton and Allied Textiles Industries (EUROCOTON); and

Fair Wear Foundation (FWF). We have consulted the websites of all these associations and finally opted for FWF to select cases for our research. FWF is an international verification initiative dedicated to enhancing workers' lives all over the world, and as such the only association above with an explicit focus on aspects of sustainability. Herewith, it is important to mention that the FWF focuses on the social aspects of producing and providing textile products, such as: freedom of choice of employment, prohibition of child labour, and safe and healthy working conditions. Ecological aspects of sustainability are not prioritised in the strategy of FWF. However, by consulting the websites of the Belgian and Dutch members of the FWF, we have observed that many of these enterprises address both social and ecological themes.

Applying the method of serendipity, which is an accidental discovery of something valuable (Pina e Cunha et al., 2010; Foster & Ford, 2003), several enterprises were identified as being interesting for this research: C&A, Orimpex, Fair 21, Cora Kemperman, G-Star Raw, H&M, Inditex Group (Zara), JBC, Kuyichi Europe, and GroeneWas. Furthermore, we included all Belgian and Dutch enterprises that are members of Fair Wear Foundation. For Belgium, these enterprises are ACP, Mayerline, Sparkling Ideas, and Stanley & Stella. There are 36 Dutch enterprises associated with Fair Wear Foundation. In total, we obtained a list of 50 enterprises, producing and/or selling clothes. After having a closer look at the websites of the enterprises and their CSR reports, 27 enterprises were selected because of their record in sustainability. After contacting them, five companies were willing to participate in the research.

Primary data was collected by semi-structured interviews. The semi-structured interview is a strong tool for studying industrial networks (Easton, 2007) and, thus, suitable for the fashion industry. This ensures that there is a certain standard as a starting point. It also increases the possibility that the cases can be compared. The semi-structured interviews were carried out at the location of the organisation, so that the interviewee was in his or her natural environment. The interviewees all gave permission to use the name of the enterprise as well as their personal names in this article. Secondary data from websites, CSR reports, and ratings of agencies which were at our disposal were used to give input in the interview but also to confirm or disconfirm what was claimed by the interviewee.

Case studies

The five companies that responded affirmatively to our inquiries are Stanley & Stella, Orimpex, ProGarments, Mayerline, and Van de Velde.

Stanley & Stella

Stanley & Stella is a young Belgian fashion enterprise established in Brussels, January 2012. We interviewed Pieter Van Den Bossche, Marketing Manager.

This enterprise is specialised in premium print-ready and environmentally friendly fashion for the merchandising sector. Stanley & Stella combines cutting-edge, fashion-forward apparel from eco-friendly materials with a sustainable and ethical production process.

Owners and the major investor of Stanley & Stella were previously involved in B&C, a traditional fashion enterprise. Hence, the move towards sustainability indicates a conscious choice for a sustainable production process. They noticed a business opportunity of starting a sustainable brand. According to them sustainability is a concept one has to take into consideration because of the growing number of people on earth and the continuously growing consumption market.

Orimpex

Orimpex is a Dutch-Turkish enterprise that specialises in producing environmentally friendly fashion for the retail market. The production facility of Orimpex is situated in Izmir because this region is known for growing long, soft, and strong cotton fibres. Orimpex specialises in the production of fashion for babies, women, and men. We interviewed the owner, Ali Polat.

Since its establishment in 2007, Orimpex was able to double its turnover and became one of the leading fashion enterprises with a production completely based on organic cotton and bamboo.

The founder of Orimpex has been motivated by living in one of the most well-known regions growing organic cotton, i.e. Izmir in western Turkey. This company would not have started if the founder were not inspired by sustainability from the beginning of his project. Orimpex attaches great importance to certification in order to improve the reliability of its products. Orimpex strives for improvement of the fair trade relations with the farmers engaged in the production process of organic cotton.

ProGarments

The beginning of ProGarments goes back to 2001. ProGarments specialises in producing work wear, swimwear, kids wear, outdoor- and sportswear. The initial idea behind the enterprise consisted in buying and selling textiles from Hong Kong. Due to dependence on the suppliers, flexibility, continuity, quality, and reliability of the production process could not always be guaranteed, which sparked ProGarments' decision to begin its own production in China. In 2010, a new plant was opened with the latest technology and machinery. The leadership is in control of the Dutch headquarter which guarantees a production process satisfying European standards.

We interviewed Bernhard Richtering Blenken, who owns the company. ProGarments started as an enterprise engaged in social aspects of sustainability. Via their membership of the Fair Wear Foundation, this engagement became more formalised and according to the interviewee ProGarments even became a pioneer among other Fair Wear members. Due to customer requests, ProGarments also introduced organic cotton and recycled polyester in their production.

ProGarments is a trendsetter in new materials such as recycled polyester and organic cotton. Their business strategy is based on the triple bottom line. According to the owner of ProGarments the enterprise continuously strives to respect the environment to a maximum level and, therefore, emphasises the following aspects of sustainability: reducing water, air, and soil pollution, as well as the emission of sound; prevention, control, and reduction of residual material and runoff; and the deliberate choice of raw materials, resources, and sustainable machinery.

Mayerline

Mayerline, a Belgian family-owned business specialised in women's fashion, was founded in 1957 by Joseph Mayer and his wife Jeanne Vrydags. At first the clothes were sold on the market. Later, Mayerline developed into an enterprise with shops, 'shop in shops' in branches of the shopping mall Galeria Inno and being present in multi-brand shops. Mayerline also owns a branch in Lithuania which opened in 1999. Mayerline sells its collections in Belgium, as well as in The Netherlands. We interviewed Marc Faber, brand consultant.

Mayerline focuses on issues such as: no child labour, reasonable wages, and safe working conditions. Mayerline only cooperates with suppliers that respect the sustainability policy of Mayerline itself.

Sustainability issues penetrated Mayerline from day one of the existence of this fashion enterprise. The founder sensitised his own children and employees with respect to sustainability issues such as sorting out their waste and being economical with the use of water and energy. Transmission of sustainable values continued through the next generations. While sustainability was something that Mayerline always found to be very important, the outside world was not aware of the efforts Mayerline took towards sustainability. This situation was made clear by the negative evaluation Mayerline received by 'Schone kleren' in 2009, an network organisation in Belgium of different NGOs that urges for better working conditions in the clothing industry worldwide. From this moment on Mayerline invested in making its sustainability policy transparent to the public and became a member of the Fair Wear Foundation. In this way, Mayerline started formalising its sustainability policy and made progressive steps towards becoming a more sustainable enterprise.

Van de Velde

The Belgian company Van de Velde was founded in 1919 by Achiel and Margaretha Van de Velde. From this moment on, Van de Velde continuously implemented a strategy of expansion and in 1997 the decision was made to introduce 40% of its shares on the stock market Euronext Brussels. This expansion strategy resulted in the presence of Van de Velde in countries such as Germany,

China, USA, Spain, The Netherlands, the UK, and Tunisia. We interviewed Valery Ameel, Quality Manager. Van de Velde is one of the major players in producing and retailing lingerie in Belgium.

As its core business Van de Velde creates, produces and commercialises luxurious lingerie with brand names such as Marie-Jo, Marie-Jo L'Avonture, Marie-Jo Intense, Prima Donna, Prima Donna Twist, and Andres Sarda. The key activities are situated in Belgium, i.e. design and product development, prototypes, contact with suppliers and purchasing strategy, controlling fabrics, cutting fabrics, end control, administration, distribution, sales, and marketing. Van de Velde mainly uses European resources which are prepared in Belgium and assembled in foreign production branches.

From the beginning, Van de Velde made an effort to be an enterprise applying social and environmental responsibility. Under pressure from the trade union, Van de Velde extended its social responsibility programme which took shape in the SA 8000 certificate. After implementing SA 8000, Van de Velde realised that this implementation contributed to the welfare of the entire organisation and voluntarily expanded the social side of sustainability. From an environmental point of view, Van de Velde started to implement Ökotex standards to protect the health of its customers. Van de Velde realises that the fashion industry evolves towards more sustainable production and understands the need to join this evolution.

Results and discussion

Sustainability record

From an outside perspective one has to rely on external sources to define the sustainability record of companies. Websites of the companies or their CSR reports must be verified with other information such as membership in sustainability-driven organisations and sustainability-related certificates. We do not distinguish between certificates and associations, since associations such as FWF also conduct audits for their members and, therefore, can be seen as providing some kind of external certificate. Table 1 summarises this evidence in relation to sustainability. We made a distinction between relevant certificates and organisations that focus on social, environmental and both social and environmental aspects. Fair Wear Foundation (FWF); Business Social Compliance (BSCI) and SA8000 focus mainly on social aspects. FWF is a non-profit organisation that works with companies in the garment industry to improve the working conditions. The basis is formed by their 'code of labour practices'. BSCI is a business-driven initiative for companies launched by the Foreign Trade Association. Their approach is to unite companies around one common code of conduct and to help their members into building a more ethical supply chain.

SA8000 is recognized worldwide as being an auditable social certification for decent workplaces. GOTS, the Global Organic Textile Standard, is a leading standard worldwide for textiles made from organic fibres. It is the only one from the selection we made which requires compliance with environmental and social criteria. Two standards have been selected that relate to the environment. Organic Content Standard (OCS), formerly Organic Exchange, is a standard that aims to verify the content of organically grown materials in a final product. Oeko-Tex is a certification system to test textiles for harmful substances.

All cases subscribe to and implement measures targeting the *social* dimension of sustainability. The cases are members of FWF, BSCI or have been certified by SA8000. Van de Velde is the only fashion enterprise in Belgium and The Netherlands that has obtained this certification.

Table 1 Sustainability related certificates and associations relevant for the fashion industry

| | Social | | | Social & Environmental | Environmental | |
| | | | | | Agriculture | Chemicals |
	FWF	BSCI	SA 8000	GOTS	OCS	Öko-Tex
Stanley & Stella	X			X		X
Orimpex				X	X	
ProGarments	X	X				
Mayerline	X					
Van de Velde			X			X

Differences can be observed for the *environmental* dimension. Stanley & Stella and Orimpex are the only ones that are GOTS certified. They integrate sustainability in the entire supply chain. Orimpex has an OCS standard. The textile it uses is nearly 100% organic. ProGarments works with environmentally friendly resources, but does not consider sustainability of the entire supply chain. Van de Velde does not exclusively work with environmentally friendly resources but guarantees the safety of their clients by working with textiles that are Oeko-tex certified. Environmental concerns are not inherent to the production process of Mayerline, but are addressed in an indirect way, e.g. by choosing green energy and water purification when building a plant.

The third component of sustainability, i.e. prosperity, is not deductible from standards nor from certifications. But, each enterprise is clear about its *economic* goal, i.e. being profitable. However, the enterprises differ in the role sustainability plays in achieving this common goal. Stanley & Stella and Orimpex rely on their sustainability ideas as the way to success. Mayerline as well as Van de Velde do not use sustainability measures to generate economic value, but realise that a modern society expects enterprises to take sustainability into consideration.

These two enterprises are reflecting on the fact that sustainability may become more important as a strategic advantage in creating economic value in the near future. ProGarments sees the move towards sustainability within the fashion industry as a business opportunity.

While the founders have been aware of the sustainability principles, it is clear that Stanley & Stella and Orimpex have gone much further. They implemented sustainability in a one-phase process. This means that they integrate sustainability together with the entire business model of the enterprise. Mayerline, ProGarments, and Van de Velde followed a maturation process. In the first phase, these enterprises were occupied with several measures which can be classified as being sustainable but they did not formalise the steps they took. This formalising part happened in the second phase and can be seen as an engagement towards more sustainability in the future.

The reasons for these differences are twofold. First, Orimpex and Stanley & Stella are young and small enterprises. So, the influence of the leader of the enterprise is much stronger than in larger enterprises such as Mayerline and Van de Velde. New ideas are gradually adopted. Indeed, the role of an ethically engaged leader is crucial for implementing sustainability within an enterprise (Taubitz, 2010). Moreover, while there is an ongoing discussion on the impact of the company size on innovation, other studies seem to suggest that smaller enterprises exhibit higher levels of dynamic innovation performance (Stock et al., 2002). Second, Mayerline and Van de Velde have been in existence for much longer than Orimpex and Stanley & Stella. The norms and values in the beginning period were different from the concept of sustainability we know nowadays. The basis of these norms and values are possibly the same, but today the choices are made much more explicit.

Role of emerging Davids and greening Goliaths in transforming the fashion industry

Determining the cases as emerging Davids or greening Goliaths

To evaluate whether the participating companies should be considered as 'Davids' or as 'Goliaths' we used the criteria by Hockerts and Wüstenhagen (2010). For an emerging David the enterprise should be younger than 15 years old; the CEO must be younger than 50, and the company should be privately owned and managed by the CEO. Table 2 gives an overview of the five cases.

Based on these criteria, Orimpex and ProGarments should be considered as 'Davids'. Stanley & Stella is a young enterprise run by a young CEO and hence we consider Stanley & Stella as a 'David', despite the fact that it is only partially owned by the CEO. Mayerline and Van de Velde are considered as 'Goliaths'. They do not satisfy the requirements, especially because they are older than 15 years.

Table 2 Corporate data of the participating enterprises based on Hockerts and Wüstenhagen's (2010) criteria for being an emerging 'David'

	Year of foundation of the company	Age of the CEO	Company owned and managed by CEO
Stanley & Stella	2012	40	partially
Orimpex	2007	35	yes
ProGarments	2001	40	yes
Mayerline	1957	40	partially
Van de Velde	1919	53	partially

Competition

When interested in influencing aspects of sustainable policies on the fashion sector, an inevitable question is how players in this industry experience competition. Stanley & Stella is strongly aware of its competitors. Stanley & Stella considers every player in the entire fashion sector as a competitor on the condition that they consider themselves as being a sustainable enterprise. They do not perceive themselves as being unique in the market. They even label some of these players as 'industrial spies'. There are also advantages of not being the only player in the market. Stanley & Stella is inspired by other enterprises like Patagonia, a successful American enterprise which, according to Stanley & Stella, is *the* reference of sustainability within the fashion industry.

A totally different picture of the fashion market can be found at Orimpex, which claims to have no competition at all in The Netherlands. The only three competitors in Turkey do not even work in a fully sustainable way. Therefore, Orimpex perceives itself as a unique player. Orimpex handles a narrow frame of reference, on the one hand, because Orimpex only focuses on the Dutch and the Turkish market which can be a dangerous strategy in a globalising world, and on the other hand, because Orimpex only uses organic cotton and recycled polyester as resources for its collection while other enterprises are also implementing sustainability measures, but do not exclusively focus on these measures.

ProGarments is not very clear in its vision on competition in relation to sustainable fashion enterprises. ProGarments believes that the fashion sector is not a very attractive one for an enterprise to start implementing sustainability policies because the investments associated with them are a major financial risk.

It is also possible to be aware of competitors on the sustainability-orientated fashion market while not having a clear frame of reference. This is the case with Mayerline, which communicates clearly against whom it is competing.

Van de Velde knows who its competitors are. However, this does not affect the sustainability policies of Van de Velde which claims to operate autonomously from other enterprises in the sector.

Knowledge sharing

Knowledge transfer can be seen as a basis for influencing the mass market (Schaltegger, 2002). Therefore, we investigated how knowledge sharing is perceived by the selected cases.

One way of collecting knowledge, inspiration, or expanding a network is participating at seminars or conferences. Stanley & Stella is not willing to share its own ideas with other enterprises who might be interested in its working method. This attitude also holds for Orimpex and ProGarments. Yet Orimpex makes an exception when there is a common goal. This situation occurred in the past with the development of an environmentally friendly way of packaging. One enterprise that is very clear in its unwillingness to share its knowledge is ProGarments. However, since ProGarments targets enterprises as its clients, it would welcome the growth of sustainability awareness among enterprises.

In the case of Mayerline, it is hard to speak of knowledge sharing. Despite being a member of the Fair Wear Foundation, Mayerline does not indicate possibilities of knowledge sharing with other Fair Wear Foundation members.

Van de Velde does not even consider that there could be something like knowledge sharing with the fashion sector. Van de Velde does cooperate with think tanks like Centexbel in order to improve its products and supply chain.

In general, readiness to share knowledge with potential competitors is very low. Reasons for not sharing knowledge, is to protect their knowledge and obtain competitive advantage from it.

Process of influence

Stanley & Stella does not perceive itself as being unique. It strongly rebels against major enterprises that often make mutual concessions and therefore forget about their sustainability agenda. These major enterprises sell their products with a sustainable label while, in reality, their products are not really sustainable. This situation frustrates Stanley & Stella. They find it difficult to balance social and environmental convictions with commercial considerations. Their awareness of competitors on the fashion market does not divert them from being confident about the sustainability principles Stanley & Stella handles. Therefore, Stanley & Stella wants to avoid being seen as a pioneer or a follower. However, the owner realises that they are an enterprise strongly based on sustainability, which creates an image of being an influencer in the fashion sector.

A completely different perception of uniqueness is noted at Orimpex. Being GOTS certified, using organic cotton, and the introduction of recycled polyester are reasons for perceiving themselves as a unique player in the fashion industry. However, Orimpex does not intend to be in this position and, therefore, does not apply a specific strategy nor has the need to constantly improve itself in sustainability engagement in order to keep its position. Orimpex claims to not be aware of competitors. Starting as a producer and seller of sustainable fashion was a difficult process. Challenges in this process were making the organic clothing more fashionable, working in a fragmented market, and stimulating farmers to proceed with growing organic cotton. This resulted in seeing itself as not being influenced by competitors in implementing a sustainability programme. Orimpex perceives itself as an influencer of the fashion industry because it entered the market as a sustainable player, introducing fashionable colours in organic cotton and starting a collection based on recycled polyester.

ProGarments clearly experiences itself as a unique player in the niche of work wear and, therefore, considers itself as an innovator aiming at influencing the market. It perceives itself as a proactive member of the FWF and is motivated to act beyond the conditions that the FWF imposes on members and tries to work as transparently as possible. The initial reason ProGarments started working with organic cotton and recycled polyester was because of a request by Yamaha, which can be seen as an influencing factor. However, Yamaha is a client, not a competitor. ProGarments classifies itself as an influencer by producing environmentally friendly clothing. An important reason for this positioning is winning the Corporate Fashion Awards in 2012. It is expected that other players in the fashion sector will become inspired by ProGarments and, therefore, will start working in a sustainable way. ProGarments wants to sensitise multinationals to become more sustainable by purchasing work wear that is produced in a sustainable manner.

An enterprise that positions itself as being unique in work methods is Mayerline because of its stepwise approach in improving business. However, Mayerline's step-by-step approach is not directly linked to sustainability measures. Mayerline perceives its position in fashion as an influencer in general. They do invest in long-term, sustainable relationships with their suppliers and are not willing to pursue 'fast money'. Mayerline wants to focus on simple interventions that stimulate sustainability. It is assumed that they influence competitors in a direct and indirect way, but do not classify themselves as being influenced by competitors. They started formalising their sustainability policy when being negatively evaluated by an external organisation which can be seen as an influencing factor.

Van de Velde fits a dominant self-image. Its position in the fashion sector concerning producing and retailing lingerie can be seen as insular and thus unique. It does not adapt its strategy by the influence of other players on the market. Yet Van de Velde is being influenced by the trade union in implementing SA 8000. Van de Velde claims a pioneering role towards other lingerie enterprises. This role is initiated by the continuous expansion strategy since the startup of the enterprise. This dominant position of Van de Velde gives it an influencing role towards other fashion enterprises with whom Van de Velde competes.

Conclusion

Looking back at our research on the influence of sustainable fashion enterprises within the fashion sector, we can decompose the concept of influence in sustainability policies in two parts. On the one hand, there is the incoming influence. None of the enterprises wants to admit that it is influenced by its competitors. All were examples of influence in a non-competition spectrum. Therefore, on first sight, one could conclude that there is no influence of sustainable issues derived from competitors. On the other hand, there is an outgoing influence caused by enterprises themselves. Each selected case positions itself as being an influencer for competitors in the sustainable fashion industry. Here we think of examples like Van de Velde that fulfils a leading role in the joint committee of the lingerie sector; Orimpex states that being an influencer in sustainable fashion is caused by making organic-based collections more fashionable; and ProGarments wants to sensitise other companies to choose for more sustainability within their daily chores.

Yet we note that these two outcomes stated above are contradictory. The selected cases are not being influenced by their competitors but, on the other hand, each enterprise profiles itself as being an influencer for their competitors. The question is: How we can explain such a contradiction? All the cases are still far from being the trigger to transform the clothing industry into a sustainable sector. To be able to influence the sector towards a sustainable transition, firms have to build partnerships with fashion companies, more specifically with Davids in the sector to be able to evolve together. None of the selected cases referred to co-evolving processes with competitors to transform the fashion industry. This is difficult because then they will have to share knowledge which might endanger their competitive context. The emphasis is still too much on competition instead of co-creation. Fashion companies will have to be guided in seeing collaboration as a key resource in their business model canvas.

References

Árnadóttir, S. Y. (2011, January). Tailoring Responses: How the Icelandic Fashion Industry Employ Strategies in a Response to CSR Pressures. 78. Copenhagen, Denmark.

Atuahene-Gima, K., & De Luca, L. M. (2008). Marketing's lateral influence strategies and new product team comprehension in high-tech companies: A cross-national investigation. *Industrial Marketing Management, 37,* 664-676.

Cohen, B., & Winn, M. (2007). Market imperfections, opportunity, and sustainable entrepreneurship. *Journal of Business Venturing, 22*(1), 29-49.

Crals, E., & Vereeck, L. (2005). The affordability of sustainable entrepreneurship certification for SMEs. *International Journal of Sustainable Development & World Ecology, 12,* 173-183.

De Prins, M., Devooght, K., Janssens, G., & Molderez, I. (2009). *Maatschappelijk verantwoord ondernemen. Van strategische visie tot operationele aanpak.* Antwerpen: De Boeck.

Department for Environment, Food and Rural Affairs. (2010, 1). *Sustainable Clothing Action Plan (update Feb 2010).* Retrieved 2012, from http://www.defra.gov.uk/publications/files/pb13206-clothing-action-plan-100216.pdf

Du, S., Bhattarchaya, C. B., & Sen, S. (2010). Maximizing Business Returns to Corporate Social Responsibility (CSR): The Role of CSR Communication. *International Journal of Management Reviews, 12*(1), 8-19.

Dworkin, R. (2003). Equality, Luck and Hierarchy. *Philosophy& Public Affairs, 31*(2), 190-198.

Easton, G. (2007). Case Research as a Methodology for Industrial Networks; A Realist Apologia. *Network dynamics in international marketing*, 73-87.

Esty, D. C., Simmons, P. J., & Price-Thomas, P. (2011). *The Green to Gold Business Playbook: How to Implement Sustainability Practices for Bottom-Line Results in Every Business Function.* John Wiley & Sons.

Foster, A., & Ford, N. (2003). Serendipity and information seeking: an empirical study. *Journal of Documentation* (Vol. 59 Iss: 3), pp.321 - 340.

Goodpaster, K. E. (2004, March/April). Ethics or excellence? Conscience as a check on the unbalanced pursuit of organisational goals. *Ivey Business Journal, 68*(4), 1-8.

Goodpaster, K. E. (2007). *Conscience and Corporate Culture.* Oxford: Blackwell Publishing.

Hale, A. and Shaw, L. M. (2001), Women Workers and the Promise of Ethical Trade in the Globalised Garment Industry: A Serious Beginning? *Antipode, 33* (3), 510–530.

Hockerts, K., & Wüstenhagen, R. (2010). Greening Goliaths versus emerging Davids: Theorizing about the role of incumbents and new entrants in sustainable entrepreneurship. *Journal of Business Venturing, 25*, 481-492.

Huanga, B., Shia, X., Yua, D., Öbornb, I., Blombäckb, K., Pagellac, T. F., et al. (2006). Environmental assessment of small-scale vegetable farming systems in peri-urban areas of the Yangtze River Delta Region, China. *Agriculture, Ecosystems & Environment, 112*(4), 391–402.

ISO (2010). ISO 26000. Guidance on social responsibility.

Joergens, C. (2006). Ethical fashion: myth or future trend? *Journal of Fashion Marketing and Management, 10*(3), 360 - 371.

Juliet, B. (2005). Schor Prices and quantities: Unsustainable consumption and the global economy. *Ecological Economics, 55*, 309 – 320.

Jussim, L., & Osgood, W. D. (1989, June). Influence and Similarity Among Friends: An Integrative Model Applied to Incarcerated Adolescents. *Social Psychology Quarterly, 52*(2), 98-112.

Kawamura, Y. (2006). Japanese Teens as Producers of Street Fashion. *Current Sociology, 54*(5), 784–801.

Laitala, K., & Boks, C. (2012). Sustainable clothing design: use matters. *Journal of Design Research, 10*(1-2), 121-139.

Lubin, D. A., & Esty, D. C. (2010, May). The sustainability imperative. *Harvard Business Review, 50*.

Norberg-Bohm, V. (2010). Creating Incentives for Environmentally Enhancing Technological Change: Lessons From 30 Years of U.S. Energy Technology Policy. *Technological Forecasting and Social Change, 65*(2), 125-148.

Pina e Cunha, M., Clegg, S. R., & Mendonça, S. (2010). On serendipity and organizing. *European Management Journal, 28*, 319-330.

Schaltegger, S. (2002). A Framework for Ecopreneurship: Leading Bioneers and Environmental Managers to Ecopreneurship. *Greener Management International, 38*, 45-58.

Soeteman, L. S. (2010, June). *Fashion in the face of culture: How do cultural influences affect fashion marketing strategies in a globalizing world? An East versus West perspective.* Bachelor Thesis, University of Tilburg, Tilburg.

Stock, G. N., Greis, N. P. & Fischer, W. A. (2002). Firm size and dynamic technological innovation. *Technovation, 22*, 537-549.

Swanson, D. L. (2008). Top Managers as Drivers for Corporate Social Responsibility. In A. Crane, *The Oxford Handbook of Corporate Social Responsibility* (Vol. 10, pp. 227-249). Oxford Handbooks.

Van Marrewijk, M. & Werre, M. (2003). Multiple Levels of Corporate Responsibility. *Journal of Business Ethics, 44*, 107-119.

Taubitz, M. (2010, May). Lean, Green & Safe. Integrating safety into the lean, green and sustainability movement. *Professional Safety, 55*(5), 39-46.

Vennemo, H., Aunan, K., Lindhjem, H., & Seip, H. M. (2009). Environmental Pollution in China: Status and Trends. *Review of Environmental Economics and Policy, 3*(2), 209-230.

Weilenmann, U., Ramírez, C., & Vanderheyden, P. (2010). Toward a 'Green' Observatory. In D. R. Silva, A. B. Peck, & B. T. Soifer (Ed.), *Observatory Operations: Strategies, Processes, and Systems III.*

Yin, R. K. (1981, March). The Case Study Crisis: Some Answers. *Administrative Science Quarterly, 26*(1), 58-65.

DOI: [10.9774/GLEAF.5001.2015.ma.00010]

Case Study

Miranda Brown Limited and the Passion to Make Fashion Sustainable[*]

Kate Kearins and Helen Tregidga
Auckland University of Technology, New Zealand

Eva Collins
University of Waikato, New Zealand

New Zealander Miranda Brown had a passion for 'beautiful things made in better ways'. She designed high-end fashion, lifestyle fashion and homeware. Combining artisan and modern techniques to produce unique fabrics, Miranda outsourced short-run production locally, and sold items to stores. Without the investment partner she needed to fund extra staff and a big marketing push, Miranda was faced with decisions about how she might reorganise her affairs so as to sustain herself, her business and her hope for sustainable fashion. In 2008, she had brought her business back to her home, and rebuilt momentum. In 2012, she took on a major campaign effort to bring customers a T-shirt made of organic cotton, plant dyed and vegetable printed with Miranda's artwork, promoting a 'Free the Sea' message. She wanted all contributors along the supply chain paid a fair wage, and a charitable donation made on the sale of each T-shirt. Again, Miranda's resources were stretched to the maximum. She had tried out different business models over the years, and she wondered whether she had an immediate future in sustainable fashion. Beyond the hard work and inspiration, it would take customers who were prepared to change their consumption models.

- Sustainability
- Fashion
- High ideals
- Limited resources

[*] The assistance of Miranda Brown with interviews in 2007 and 2008 is gratefully acknowledged. A variety of media and web sources also informed the writing of the case. Unless otherwise noted, all quotations in the case are from interviews with Miranda Brown directly. Faculty can apply for the teaching note on this case by contacting Greenleaf at http://www.greenleaf-publishing.com/default.asp?ContentID=14

Kate Kearins is Professor of Management and Deputy Dean in the Faculty of Business and Law at Auckland University of Technology, New Zealand. Her research interests are in business and sustainability, stakeholder engagement and collaboration.

✉ Faculty of Business and Law, Auckland University of Technology, Business and Law School, AUT City Campus, Auckland 1142, New Zealand

💻 Kate.kearins@aut.ac.nz

Helen Tregidga is an Associate Professor in Accounting in the Faculty of Business and Law at Auckland University of Technology, New Zealand. Her research interests are primarily related to the interface of business, society and the natural environment.

✉ Accounting Department, Auckland University of Technology, Business and Law School, AUT City Campus, Auckland 1142, New Zealand

💻 helen.tregidga@aut.ac.nz

Eva Collins is an Associate Professor in the Strategy and Human Resource Management Department at the University of Waikato. Her area of research is business strategy related to sustainability. She is an award-winning writer of sustainability case studies.

✉ Strategy and Human Resource Management Department, University of Waikato Private Bag 3105, Hamilton, New Zealand

💻 evacolln@waikato.ac.nz

We live in cataclysmic times, says Miranda Brown—designer, artisan and activist for sustainable fashion. 'Are we all going to end up wearing jeans and sneakers?' she asks, exasperated. She refers to the 'costume international' made in a sweatshop probably not near you... 'Are we all going to be this homogenous, non-thinking McDonald's-eating carbon-burning mass?' (Daniell, 2007)

NEW ZEALAND TEXTILE ARTIST AND designer, Miranda Brown, was on the record as saying 'sustainability, environment and humanity are at the heart of our creative practice'. Through her business, Miranda Brown Limited, she had sought to bring her passion for sustainable design to the generally fickle world of fashion. She worked 'to create timeless, beautiful objects across clothing and homeware, to adorn the body, to love the body and to bring colour into the home'. There had been at least two major decision points in the life of her business. In 2008, after entering her business in the Sustainable Business Network's Get Sustainable Challenge,[1] she sought an outside investor to enable the business to develop and expand in line with her sustainability ideals. She had found it difficult, however, to convince others to buy into her dream of 'a design-led business that values nature first'. Dejected, she decided to take time out to re-energise, but customers continued to call and the business slowly bounced back. In 2012, after winning a commendation in the Northern Sustainable Business Network awards, Miranda committed to taking customers on the journey 'of how [their] "cradle-to-cradle" T-shirt was made'.[2] Her passion for contributing to the world of slow fashion—and supporting other environmental causes—had stretched her personal resources and energy levels to the max. Was it time to step back again?

Background

Miranda Brown launched her own fashion label in 2002. With her design business starting out and staying quite small, for a time she had rented a design studio in Auckland, New Zealand's largest city.[3] In 2008, the business comprised Miranda herself, a full-time staff member and two other part-timers, but by 2012 it was mainly just Miranda fronting the business. Production was

---

1 This challenge involved completing a self-assessment of the sustainability practices of the business with some support from a Sustainable Business Network representative together with entry into regional and potentially national sustainable business awards. See www. sustainable.org.nz/cms1/index.php?page=gsc

2 Miranda Brown Conscious Cloth, Free the sea T-shirt campaign http://www.mirandabrown.co.nz/Free_The_Sea/About_this_T-shirt.htm. Accessed 1 July 2012.

3 Auckland was New Zealand's main commercial city with a regional population of more than 1.5 million of the country's 4.2 million inhabitants.

outsourced locally. Miranda Brown designs sold mainly within the domestic market. In the past there had also been some sales into neighbouring Australia where Miranda had hired the services of a part-time sales agent, as well as to a couple of North American stores.

At its peak, the Miranda Brown label embraced a full range of 'high-end, limited edition women's fashion' apparel, a 'lifestyle range' of knitwear for women, men, children and babies, and some 'homeware and accessory' items, such as cushions and scarves. The major focus was on stylish clothing for women from 'funky casual to edgy suits' (Bond, 2006). While somewhat more trendy than strictly classical, all Miranda Brown items were designed to be more than one-season wonders. Miranda aimed to produce high quality, artistically designed items that clients would want to keep, wear and enjoy for a long time.

Miranda remained very busy with management, oversight of operations, domestic sales, and the all-important design side of the business. Exhibit 1 details the process from the designs to the finished items, the people responsible and the embedded design principles. Despite her absolutely central and foundational role, Miranda claimed she was never short of ideas. Her desire to understand deeper connections had inspired her to read widely about sustainability. Her vision was broad and potentially far-reaching: she wanted her business and label to prosper on the basis of strong sustainability principles, and for these principles to connect with customers so as to contribute to a sustainable world.

Exhibit 1 Miranda Brown Limited: Efforts towards sustainable fashion 2007/08

Process	People responsible	Embedded design principles
Inspiration	Miranda Brown	Time out in nature
Artwork and drawings of designs	Miranda Brown	Natural motifs
Decisions on the collection and potential environmental NGO sponsorship	Miranda Brown	Coherence, a story, giving back to nature
Design of garments and selection/adaption of earlier styles	Miranda Brown	Timelessness and durability
Fabric selection and dyeing	Miranda Brown and full-time staff member	Natural fibre and non-toxic materials, moving towards organic dyes; dyeing outdoors to ensure fresh air ventilation
Pattern cutting	Part-time staff members	Recycling paper, minimal waste
Making up of samples	Part-time staff members	Minimal waste, offcuts when possible recut into baby range; any further unneeded fabric donated to local communities for further creative life such as Christmas cards
Photo shoots	Outsourced	Electronic images where possible
Catalogue coordination	Miranda Brown	Initial print run with reorders only if needed
Sales to existing and new stores	Miranda Brown and full-time staff member in New Zealand Part-time sales agent in Australia	Emphasis on high quality, New Zealand-made garments from natural fibres Personal contact to communicate the design principles
Production and dispatch	Miranda Brown coordinated a group of local outworkers or outsourced to Auckland-based Cut-Make-and-Trim organisations	As above for making up of samples Ethics, health and safety issues always considered in choice of manufacturers Unbleached paper packaging used to freight items to retail outlets Offshore shipments made once a year
Supporting activities e.g. design studio management, HRM, budgeting and finance, brand awareness, publicity, website and design installations, involvement in Trash to Fashion event as trustee	Miranda Brown	Fair-trade products for all consumables and energy efficiency practices in the studio, commitment to a low emissions vehicle and carbon neutrality through offsetting

Starting with nature-inspired design

Miranda believed that sustainability started with a fundamental design ethos. 'First of all, we are nature... Nature inspires me, how it touches my soul, and my heart, it's the reason I do what I do, I guess'. She loved to walk and spend time in the natural environment. 'When I start designing, I need to be free in nature. Because...you can feel everything drop away...you find yourself surrendered. And then you can start creating'.

Miranda saw her work as akin to telling a story with fabrics and design. She generally transferred the motifs of one design across different items in a particular collection. Sometimes she used line drawings and other times block printing designs, along with more sophisticated techniques. She had worked with motifs that had a strong 'iconic New Zealand kind of feel' but also with more Pacific-derived print motifs, often based on native fauna and flora (see www. mirandabrown.co.nz/Fashion.htm for examples of Miranda's fashion designs). Some Asian influences could be detected in her work. She also drew her inspiration more widely. Miranda described some of her designs:

> This motif here...it's sacred geometry in actual fact, but it's got that form, Marama [moon], the frangipani [flower], and so people in New Zealand relate to it, but also, there's an international context. And that's talking about our connectedness, that we are all one, so let's get on and have a good time as opposed to warring and fighting.
>
> ...The lotus was a lovely collection I did. That T-shirt was really popular, one of my little drawings.

Another design included tiny stars:

> That went right across [the range]... We did that on beautiful tailored coats... And that story was about the stars, and...that's how far I go into a collection—I was studying the cosmos, I was reading Stephen Hawking's [book on the] 'Big Bang Theory',[4] and the notion 'we are stardust', you know it just fascinated me. Oh my God, we are stardust, how magical. And you start to research how life form has come about, and it gets really, really interesting... I'm just doing it to share stories with people.

Miranda had become increasingly conscious of issues around resource use and waste: 'I'm gracious for using the resources that come from this planet, that's why I respect them, and the processes—how we recycle our waste, or we try not to create waste...the use of the materials, and the disposing of them'. These were all aspects she wanted her business to focus more on, but the small business did not have formal systems to measure and evaluate progress on these fronts. She had entered the Sustainable Business Network's Get Sustainable Challenge in 2007 as an opportunity to reflect on the sustainability challenges facing her business, and point to where progress had already been made.

---

4 Stephen Hawking's (1998) bestseller, *A Brief History of Time: From the Big Bang to Black Holes*, addressed questions around cosmology; that is the study of the universe as a whole—its structure, origin and development.

Beyond the accolades, three main areas of improvement were noted including: the need for a long-term business plan and monitoring financial sustainability; implementing measuring systems and carbon calculations for resource use; and continuing to advance understanding and practice of 'cradle-to-cradle' thinking. Miranda was keen for the next big push.

By early 2008, however, Miranda was left feeling her dreams had been dashed. With advice and support from a team of business experts, she had made a big pitch for an investor. With a 32 page business plan and a slick presentation, she put her business and her beliefs to the test: 'It felt like being in the dragon's den'. One potential investor had seemed ideal—a background in organics, great empathy with sustainability and success in prior business ventures ready to invest some of his capital in the right business. The answer came back 'no'. If she could not convince this fellow believer, she wondered who she could convince.

Miranda was exhausted and took a break...but the phones kept ringing for re-orders of some popular items in the women's wear range, her merino wool lifestyle garments in particular, and the hand dyed silk lifestyle pieces. She began to wonder whether there was some lesson in what all the advisers had been saying, 'You are stretched too far, you need to focus more'. With no investor, Miranda knew she was not going to be able to afford to expand overseas, but refreshed, she started to think 'this is me doing what I do best, connecting with people at a deep level and giving them high quality garments that they love'. And 'hey local's good'. She kept going with a home-based business, and the ideal of every facet of the business being connected to 'making a positive impact on the planet' (Sustainable Business Network, 2011).

Following the design process through to finished items

Miranda's preference was to use natural fibre in her designs, which included New Zealand wool and imported silk, linen and cotton. She claimed,

> A lot of polyplastic fabrics have damaging effects in the production process, so to eliminate them from the collection is great... Ten thousand people die each year from pesticides associated with cotton growing in Third World countries, so we don't want to be a part of that.

Wool was one of her favourite materials, with Miranda estimating about 60–70% of the designs used it: 'That all starts out cream. And we hand dye it and print it, and we use water based printing inks, that are very, very low toxicity'. Bamboo, hemp and linen were other examples of sustainable fibre Miranda included in her future thinking, but merino (a type of fine wool) remained popular because of its beauty and durability.

Acid fabric dyes sourced from Germany had proven to be very effective in adhering to the materials through sustained wear and washing, according to

Miranda. She sought softer dyes and looked to organic dyes. A labour-intensive ancient *shibori* resist dye technique Miranda had studied in Japan was used to add colour and motifs. She combined traditional techniques with modern technologies including laser cutting and other digital applications. 'You're constantly having to look at the way you can engineer things—a line of material might finish, so you have to find out a new source, and different technologies'.

Miranda's musings, drawings and designs formed the basis of her collections. Her designs were known for their use of 'bold colour and strong repeat patterns' (Bond, 2006). She had 'made a radical change within the relentless industry of fashion by producing one collection per year' rather than one for summer and one for winter as before. She had opted for lifestyle winter/trans-season fashion which could be worn for longer each year. She designed so as to minimise waste as well as to reuse and recycle, ordering fabrics in only the amounts required, with any surplus made into baby wear, incorporated in other lines, or donated to school groups (Sustainable Business Network, 2011). Sometimes Miranda had help cutting the patterns and making up samples which then went into the photo shoots for the Miranda Brown Limited catalogue. Selling the collection to store buyers or direct to customers was the next phase.

Like many other design businesses, Miranda Brown Limited outsourced production of clothing and homeware orders. Miranda herself co-ordinated a group of outworkers to make the garments or otherwise used local Cut, Make and Trim organisations, known in the rag trade as a CMT. Miranda saw New Zealand as a '"boutiquey" kind of manufacturing country' where short runs like hers were all that could be managed cost-effectively. She was happy to keep her manufacturing close by, where she could keep her eye on maintaining high quality. Local production within New Zealand was supported by excellent, short-run production and adaptability—and was generally well regarded for the quality of the garments produced (Fashion Industry New Zealand, 2005a). However small enterprises often complained about the high occupational safety and health requirements and compulsory costs on employers for accident cover (Fashion Industry New Zealand, 2005b). Manufacturing costs in New Zealand's Western style economy were on average much higher overall than in lower labour cost countries with less stringent regulations.

Miranda had said she was not interested in having her designs manufactured in China:

> Environmentally, [she claimed] it's just another nail in the coffin... When we do this we are taking work away from New Zealanders, we are removing the manufacturing base which is really hard to grow again... And in China the human rights conditions are not good. It's also a pollution-filled process (Daniell, 2007).

Miranda Brown Limited's aim to keep producing locally fitted well with the major thrust of Fashion Industry New Zealand, to keep manufacturing in New Zealand. That body noted, as a consequence, an almost inevitable focus for New Zealand designers not just on quality rather than quantity, but also on precision rather than price (Fashion Industry New Zealand, 2005a).

Who's buying the Miranda Brown label?

At one stage Miranda Brown Limited sold through 40 New Zealand stores across fashion, baby-wear and homeware, as well as internationally to select stores. In 2007, Miranda had devised 'MB on tour' where she met directly with her main New Zealand market though the galleries and specialist designer stores where her products were sold. In 2008, she tweaked the approach, selling direct in a couple of places through evening events with sparkling wine among gatherings of friends and customers outside the regular store locations. It was an approach she continued over the ensuing years.

> [Moving around the country] has been fantastic, because I've got to meet my client for the first time. I know who my client generally is, but I've really got to meet Mrs Smith from Hawkes Bay. And she's got and loves the jacket, and she's very stylish, and she wants the hoody and you know I've got to see lifestyles.

She saw an advantage in being tuned into the market.

> You definitely need to be listening to the market, and asking what does the market want. Now, the market always wants a scarf. You know you need to consider and respect your client, that they have a different color way, what suits them, and you need to listen to that. So we're not separated from the consumer.

Miranda saw the target market as the 30–60-year-old woman who could afford to pay above-average prices for her locally made designer products and the personal service more likely to be received in upscale boutiques and galleries. Miranda recognised her products were not always affordable. 'If people stop buying my things, it's more because they're too expensive. That is one of the dilemmas of making my products in New Zealand, with a lot of manufacturing going to China,' she said.

At the end of the first tour, Miranda had returned home more convinced than ever that the customers she had spoken to bought into the philosophy behind her label:

> People buy into the Miranda Brown label, because...[they] love my philosophy, because they're tired of vacuous consumption. Yes, everyone needs to go to Glassons[5] and get their quick merino T-shirt, because it's cheap. But people will support ideologies, I believe more and more, because we are all being asked to look at our consumption. We're all being asked you know, to think about carbon credits, miles on food...

Miranda claimed these views were becoming more common, and that she was part of a wave of businesses with vision and purpose that integrated such concerns. She felt her ideas translated well internationally into the Australian

---

5 Glassons was a chain of inexpensive women's clothing stores aimed at the younger woman. In 2012 Hallenstein Glassons Holdings owned 36 Glassons stores in New Zealand and 29 in Australia.

market, and had resonance in the small forays she had made into the United States market to date. But in both 2008 when Miranda Brown Limited failed to secure an outside investor, and continuing into 2012, the business did not have the resources for a further push into these markets.

Wanting to make deep connections with customers and beyond

Miranda saw herself as an artisan who worked with natural materials to produce objects of beauty.

> I'm an artisan, and as artisans we have existed for thousands of years... We work with minerals, fiber and we process them. We're in touch, we're very deep people. And we're in touch with the material, and we touch it and we feel it... And it's a flow, we're completely connected. So, as humans we have a desire to have beautiful objects, we create things of beauty.

She believed that people were fundamentally attracted to having beautiful things in their lives—and that by buying her designs, they could connect deeply with what was really important:

> Through my label I'm trying to educate people about universal connectedness... We are attracted to things, it's on a deep subconscious level... If you look at India and the Mandala, which I often work with in circular forms, I work with forms that take you in. And I mean if I just drew a literal tree, it could be kind of interesting, but it's not that interesting, you know. Just to have sheep on the front of a T-shirt, I mean, what is it saying? ... So the Mandala for me, it's one of my first prints, and I hand drew the circles, and that was a meditation in itself. Now, Mandala literally means circle in Hindi, and that talks about connectedness, 'we are one'... So I feel that once you know that you're actually inter-connected to the food chain, once you know you're connected to that plant, and the birds and bees and nature, oh it's a magical, amazing, biological physics journey, you really want to look after it. There's just no way that you disrespect it, and toxify it, and all of that.

Miranda saw the human obsession with materialism and having material things 'as something that we have to face' and a reason to therefore have beautiful things made in better ways. She noted that as humans,

> we've always adorned, we've always told stories through fabric. It's who we are... that's part of being human—the creating, and telling stories, that's why we have intelligence, and so let's be intelligent about what we design and how we make it in the process.

She wanted people to have products they loved and valued—and would keep for a long time. She pointed to one of her cushions—saying people would always want to pad for comfort and have colour in their lives: 'I want people to have this [cushion], and the colour you know, it's relaxing to look at, it's inspiring to look at, it has a vibration...it's soul-food'.

More and more, she felt, people would buy the kinds of products she designed because of what she called:

> the experience, that 'I'm saving the whales at the same time, as buying this object', because it's the feel-good. Because 'I'm...oh you know, oh god, I feel a bit guilty, shall I buy it, oh look, actually money from this, it's a story'. And again and again and again, it's all about the story. And it's not vacuous consumption. And...it will last you a long time. There's every reason why you will make that conscious consumer decision.

Miranda tried to pair up with environmental NGOs for some of her work. She noted,

> It makes me feel really joyous to do positive work. So that's very much become a focus for me. I haven't been able to do it every collection, but now I realize it is *my* soul food, for each collection to support a group or an organization.

Miranda saw her role in this outreach as 'to inspire the client... And the clients who are buying my clothes can afford to do that, so it's an invitation in a way'. She simply did not see people all 'wearing roman sandals and eating lentils and never buying anything again'. Rather she claimed the new green way we were stretching into was about living, working and consuming 'in a very cohesive, inclusive, we are part of nature way'.

In 2012, when Miranda launched her Free the Sea campaign, she was trying to prove a paradigm shift was possible. She had, as one reporter put it, literally taken

> the plunge into marine conservation... The launch of her Free the Sea range of tees is her bid to help the most endangered species of our watery world, including Maui's dolphins which are estimated by the [New Zealand] Conservation Department to now number about 55 (Oliver, 2012).

One of the T-shirt designs carried the Free the Sea message in big letters emblazoned across most of the front; the other designs were more subtle. Customers were encouraged to order T-shirts online—for men, women and children—that were made according to Miranda's designs, using organic dyes and print inks, in Bali from organic cotton. Miranda planned to be on hand providing up-to-date video footage during the manufacturing process.

Priced at NZ$35–55, the T-shirts represented for Miranda a leap of faith that customers would buy into the cradle-to-cradle ideal of responsible production and consumption and reuse—and that they would be prepared to pay a premium over what they paid for regular cheap T-shirts—sometimes as little as NZ$7–8—to do so. Moreover, NZ$5 (around the price of a McDonald's Big Mac in New Zealand) from every T-shirt sold automatically went to the customer's choice of one of three environmental organisations. This model really embraced the idea of slow fashion, to the extent customers might understand that term. They could order in May—and expect to receive their T-shirts by October that year. Miranda explained, 'It takes time, energy and resources to make garments and we are going to take you through this process from design to delivery'. Miranda pulled out all the stops—but by late November 2012, she was left with a huge pile of T-shirts yet to sell at the Auckland Sustainable City Showcase event. Her resources and energies were spent and she was reconsidering her future.

Miranda wanted to raise human awareness through her timeless craftwork and by allying with a cause she believed in and thought her customers would as well. She was working alongside others, but with really just herself bringing the whole thing together, she had taken on a heavy burden. She was trying to change the increasingly prevalent model of fast fashion to slow fashion and conscious social movement-allied purchase selections, reuse and recycling. As yet, there was not a lot of evidence as to how long clients were keeping and using her more up-market products, or whether having such products sated any desire for having more material goods. Taking on the T-shirt market was taking on rather a lot—even with an ideology behind it.

Trying to make money in the New Zealand fashion scene

Miranda characterised the New Zealand fashion scene as 'kind of competitive'. Her label had only ever sold in relatively 'small volumes, it's very "boutiquey". Australia is completely saturated, and it's getting a harder and harder market [to sell into] unless you have big marketing budgets'. On the other hand, fashion chains from Australia were seen as dominating New Zealand's prime commercial real estate, having brought with them a culture of aggressive discounting (Fashion Industry New Zealand, 2007). More Australian firms had come into the New Zealand market. 'There's just more and more competition and it just squeezes the profit margins,' Miranda had lamented. Following the global financial crisis in 2008/9, New Zealand suffered a double dip recession, with retail sector sales performance and growth up across the board 5.5% in the year ending December 2011, and 5.2% for clothing, footwear and accessories (New Zealand Retailers Association, 2012).

The general consensus was that 'it's a tough market out there. Consumers have never been so spoilt for choice at every conceivable price point, nor have their expectations been so high,' noted Fashion Industry New Zealand back in 2007. Further, with select items in chain stores inching higher in both quality and price, New Zealand brands positioned in the upper middle had already found it 'a tough place to be' (Fashion Industry New Zealand, 2007). Predictions were that some well-known names in the industry would go to the wall—'no shopper is going to be loyal just because you've been around for so long and dressed their mother,' claimed one commentator speaking downunder in 2012 (Hume, 2012). Even without the current climate, investment into fashion enterprises was commonly viewed as higher risk due to the unpredictable nature of seasonal trends and shifts in consumer demand. Miranda knew after her experience in 2008 that it would be hard to find someone to invest in the business at this time—even more so one who bought into her sustainability vision with the extra costs it entailed and the low levels of revenues experienced to date. Exhibit 2 provides a summary of the business's financial performance up to 2008 and projected results given a further half a million investment to fund an operations manager, a dedicated sales manager and further working capital and branding. Without that investment, and with the many challenges and expenses of the Free the Sea T-shirt campaign, the 2012 position was assumed to be dire.

Exhibit 2 Miranda Brown Limited financial information as at 2008* (NZ$000s)

	Actual 2006/7	Actual 2007/8	Forecast 2008/9	Forecast 2009/10	Forecast 2010/11
Customers (numbers of stores)					
New Zealand and Australia	30	40	180	240	280
Other international			40	140	300
Revenues					
New Zealand and Australia	295	320	640	960	1250
Other international			160	640	1630
Gross profit	109	118	360	800	1584
Gross profit margin %	36.9	37%	45%	50%	55%
Selling, general and administrative expenses	98	97	320	560	1008
Earnings before interest, taxation, depreciation and amortisation	11	21	40	240	576

* More recent financial information is not included. Most of the information in this exhibit applies to the main narrative of the case set in 2008. It is not intended to reflect the situation in 2012, either before or after the Free the Sea T-shirt campaign, which gave Miranda cause to rethink her approach to life and business.

On the supply side, 80–90% of textiles for apparel were imported into New Zealand from Asia and Europe. The cost of these imported materials increasingly outweighed the costs of the local manufacturing processes (Fashion Industry New Zealand, 2006). Manufacturing small boutique runs was very challenging, according to Miranda who recognised the tension between keeping costs down and seeing people paid a fair wage. An industry observer commenting on Cut, Make and Trim organisations said, 'They open and they close'.[6] Inside the industry there was mention of undercutting by fly-by-nighters who were offering poor working conditions and pay, possibly to illegal immigrants

---

6 M. Smith, July 18, 2007, personal communication.

(Campbell, 2005). Miranda's response was to work with reputable firms and to attempt to focus her practice on more efficient design.

Miranda had decided not to show her designs at fashion expos, partly because of the expense and partly because past fashion shows had not really created interest in international sales for her label. She still saw New Zealand Fashion Week as an important and exciting event—but expensive and time-consuming, and only worth doing if one was fully committed and could pull in bigger international sales, which were never a certainty for the smaller players. 'It's profile, it's all of that. I'd rather create my profile through the editorial [through interviews reproduced in the media], which we have been doing and through the stories, the experiences,' she added.

The local market was, however, flooded with mass-produced overseas clothing and homeware products. Moreover, fast fashion had brought with it increased expectations of the use of industrial robotics, shorter lead times for production, increasing numbers of ranges each year and massive discounting. In general, increased demand for discount fashion resulted in increased production and increased impacts, and the lower quality clothing produced reduced the likelihood of reuse, and increased the volume thrown away (Defra, 2007). With clothing increasingly sold through chain stores there were fewer boutiques in evidence. Even then, pricier boutiques often sold overseas produced garments as well as local ones, for which they commanded higher in-store margins. Despite Miranda's wish for people to experiment beyond the 'costume internationale' of jeans, T-shirt and sneakers, there was no doubt that these items were both readily available at very competitive prices and hugely in evidence on streets downunder. New Zealand and Australian consumers followed global trends and were also prepared to buy branded products at price premiums. Only a minority could afford to pay for more expensive designer clothing—and such customers were generally neither exclusive in their buying habits nor necessarily loyal to one fashion house.

A flock of New Zealand competitors

A number of New Zealand fashion design houses had offshore presence including, among the best known, Trelise Cooper, Karen Walker, Zambesi, Nom'D, World and Kate Sylvester. Around 40 designers had showed on the catwalk at the 2012 New Zealand Fashion Week, revealing a wealth of talent, and potentially up-and-coming local designers. About half these designers sold abroad in 2008 (*The Economist*, 2008).

Miranda saw benefits for all and any New Zealand designer doing well overseas. She felt consolidation was inevitable and 'that due to New Zealand's size and resources, it must "move as a tribe"' (New Zealand Trade and Enterprise, 2004). However, the reality was that although there was no obvious internal tribal warfare, there was competition between industry members both with ideas, and within and between market segments. Designers often attempted to leverage aspects of their New Zealand heritage, incorporating 'kiwiana' icons as well as natural botanical images and Polynesian references in their designs.

A small but growing group of New Zealand designers were working more consistently with natural fibres, and could be seen as closer competitors to Miranda Brown Limited. Not only were suppliers likely to be similar, so were the potential buyers of these firms' output. One, Starfish, with founder designer, Laurie Foon and designer Carleen Schollum, having won a national Sustainable Business Award in 2007, was generally seen as ahead of Miranda Brown Limited in its sustainability practices. Starfish had been in operation since 1993 and had three New Zealand flagship stores, as well as more than 20 listed New Zealand stockists and online sales available on its website. Its garments were all New Zealand-made, its fabrics sourced within New Zealand where possible and it embraced sustainable design and production policies. Starfish also paid attention to packaging reduction and waste. Its carry bags were made from recyclable chlorine-free paper with vegetable-based ink, and surplus fabric was given to community groups. Starfish's website featured New Zealand as a rich source of inspiration and pitched enduring style 'Every Starfish garment is made to be well loved and well-worn over many seasons' (Starfish, 2013).

Another established player more particularly focused in the wool segment was Peri Drysdale with Snowy Peak and Untouched World. Drysdale had established parent company Snowy Peak in 1981 and started Untouched World in 1998. Snowy Peak operated as a specialist wholesaler of fine knitwear, and Untouched World with a broader retail concept based on high quality natural fibre fashion for both men and women, a plant extract skincare range and a homeware line. Untouched World's vision was 'through fashion to lead the way in what is possible for our planet and its people' (Untouched World New Zealand, 2007). Committed to design that minimised or eliminated harmful effects upon the environment, the company had six New Zealand stores including a flagship store in Christchurch, and sold to outlets around the world. Major brands included the award-winning Merinomink, a combination of merino fibres and possum fur[7] that was promoted as remarkably easy care. Although Untouched World was closely associated with New Zealand, manufacturing was mostly undertaken offshore. The company had produced its first sustainable development report in 2002 and had its own Untouched World Foundation dedicated to providing students with life-skills for a sustainable future. Miranda admitted to really respecting Drysdale who she saw as serving a somewhat more conservative market through Untouched World:

---

7 An introduced species, New Zealand's now 60 million plus possums were considered a major threat to native flora and fauna (including the iconic national bird, the kiwi) as well as acting as a carrier of bovine tuberculosis (infecting cattle). They were therefore considered an ecological disaster—and an ethical source of fur as the animals were widely considered as needing to be culled (Department of Conservation, 2008).

> She's fantastic. She's probably twenty years longer in the tooth than me, in terms
> of being in the industry. She had the philosophy, in terms of design, I think I have
> a jazzier story, a look about my product...literally more funky...more open-minded.

As well as stylish designs, Snowy Peak and Untouched World had developed more standard bread-and-butter lines.

Icebreaker was a major New Zealand brand which favoured the use of New Zealand wool, but it was located in the lifestyle and outdoor adventure clothing market rather than in high fashion. It had moved production from New Zealand to Asia for cost reasons, but CEO Jeremy Moon (2008) still preached sustainability. 'It's not just about where it's made; it's about how it's made,' he said when discussing his company's introduction of Baacode, a traceability system that enabled customers to trace the company's sustainability and ethical practices, beginning at the sheep farm where the wool was grown and extending right through the supply chain. Traceability was also discussed at a 2008 Fashion Industry New Zealand event in relation to 'being able to trace the journey of our clothes from the land where the fabrics are grown and milled, through to design concept, manufacturing and into the customer's wardrobe' (Brown, 2008). Miranda knew there were some formidable competitors out there, and despite the need to compete, she considered the bar would have to be raised even further for fashion to be truly sustainable. Hence her 2012 Free the Sea campaign.

Going all the way with sustainable fashion

Was there a niche for sustainable fashion, the way Miranda envisioned it? Was green really the new black? Going green had been a theme in previous New York and London fashion weeks. Although eco-friendly fashion might have brought to mind 'burlap sacks, hemp necklaces and Birkenstocks,' according to one observer, today's environmentally thoughtful designers were far more innovative and 'fashion-forward' (Unterberger, 2007). Some ecofashionistas, as they have been called, were doing much more than just pushing organic fibre lines. Fashion company Moral Fervor used a synthetic and sustainable fabric from fermented corn, donating a portion of profits to helping feed women and children. Another player, coolnotcruel, focused on labour conditions, and providing work for indigenous people with fair compensation and healthy work environments (Unterberger, 2007).

Pioneering US eco-designer Linda Loudermilk boasted a luxury eco-line of clothing and accessories based on 'sustainably produced materials from exotic plants including bamboo, sea cell soya and sasawashi'—a fabric made from a Japanese leaf that contained anti-allergen and antibacterial properties (West, 2007). She also incorporated natural themes each season, and embraced cause-related marketing supporting water rights and other initiatives. With her own eco-accreditation system, and like Miranda, an interest in communicating through the media, Loudermilk proclaimed she aimed

> to give eco glamour legs, a fabulous look and a slammin' attitude that stops traffic and shouts the message that eco could be edgy, loud, playful, feminine (or not) and hypercool. All created by meticulously researched sustainable business practices and fair labour standards (Loudermilk, 2007).

Sustainable fashion clearly took businesses beyond issues of sourcing organic raw materials, less harmful chemicals and bleaches, into recycling and reuse of textiles (recycled soda bottles were a popular choice), and into durability, fair trade and labour issues. In late 2007, WWF reported that those selling luxury or high-end brands in an increasingly resource constrained and unequal world needed to do more to justify their value (Bendell and Kleanthous, 2007). They were seen to fuel unnecessary consumption and provoke discontent among poorer members of society, in particular. Commentators had pointed to a disturbing gap between the glamour of the catwalk and the squalor of the sweatshop (Thomas, 2007). Then there were end-of-life product concerns: the average person in the United States threw away nearly 70 pounds of clothing and textiles per year, according to the US Council for Textile Recycling (Kim, 2007). Carbon footprint and life cycle analyses of products were also appearing. The UK's EarthPositive apparel had the first carbon reduction label for climate neutral apparel made using only renewable green energy generated by wind or solar power, without detrimental effects to soil, water, animals, plants, people or climate (EarthPositive, 2008). It appeared increasingly important to get independent external verification for claims regarding products' social and environmental credentials. The more Miranda read, the more there seemed to worry about. She wondered how this latest thinking could inform her tiny business on the edge of the world.[8]

Looking ahead—as visionaries do

Miranda had taught herself to be a textile artist 'because 20 years ago, there wasn't someone I knew who was doing this... This has been an amazing process. I certainly am still trying to work out how to make money out of it,' she declared. 'You know, I have my living and we're making beautiful things, and

---

8 Conceiving of New Zealand as on the edge of the world is an initiative led by Saatchi & Saatchi global chief, Kevin Roberts and consultant Brian Sweeney as a way of thinking about 'identity, people, stories, achievements and place in the world'. See www.nzedge .com Accessed 4 December 2007.

are collected by Te Papa [The National Museum of New Zealand], and you know it's all fabulous... I love it, it's my life'. Miranda saw herself as fortunate in having 'been able to realize my signature and what I care about'. Having invested in her business, she did not own her own home as most people her age did in New Zealand but said she had come to terms with that. 'What an amazing thing to do. Honestly, there are not many people that fully, fully experiment with this, and realize their artistry—and, understanding philosophy, turn that into a business practice'. That was back in 2007–8. Now in 2012, having given her all, Miranda was under no illusion that fulfilling her dreams for sustainable fashion was easy.

She had always known there was so much to do and always more she felt she should do. 'I'm sprinting, running a business on my own, being the operational manager, being the employer, and being the designer,' she admitted in 2007. Her hectic pace was not uncommon in the industry. New Zealand Trade and Enterprise creative sector manager, Paul Blomfield was reported saying:

> At the moment designers are trying to be everything—the designer and supply chain as well as looking after the marketing and logistics. As these companies grow, they are likely to look for improved business models... One idea would be to follow the Italian model, where a manufacturer buys the rights to a designer's name and helps them to market internationally. Another idea could be designers developing collections for retail chains on a royalty basis.

Design was always going to be Miranda's priority. When she bounced back in 2008 from the rebuff by the investors, she knew the business could not simply saturate the market with the same designs and expect clients to stay loyal and keep paying high prices. She drew back, thought about what was happening, and what was possible, and moved to produce her nature-inspired designs in as responsible a way as she could as essentially a solo designer working with partners for production and distribution. Miranda Brown Limited won a commendation in the trailblazer small and medium business award category at the Northern Sustainable Business Network Awards in 2011. The judges were impressed with the business's...

> ...exceptionally strong adherence to core values of sustainability, use of renewable and locally sourced materials in design of clothing, impressive clarity of stakeholders, engagement plans, and commitment to educating customers and wider marketplace (on many levels across many mediums) about sustainability, [and] strong vision and commitment to sourcing more sustainable products (Sustainable Business Network, 2011).

But those achievements were obviously not enough for Miranda. It was perhaps that last comment from the judges in 2011—the strong vision and commitment to sourcing more sustainable products—that spurred her on.

By 2012, when Miranda did the Free the Sea campaign, she wanted to take sustainable fashion to another level in New Zealand. She threw herself into yet another new business model to deliver what she called a cradle-to-cradle T-shirt. How many people would join her crusade and buy into slow fashion—a T-shirt that paid fair wages and was environmentally responsible certainly cost more, and took even the keenest customer five months from order to receipt. Would you? It was time for Miranda to step back, and refocus her energies once again.

References

Bendell, J. & Kleanthous, A. (2007). Deeper luxury: Quality and style when the world matters. www.wwf.org.uk/deeperluxury. Accessed 4 December 2007.

Bond, G. (2006, February 3). Clothed in the fabric of success. *New Zealand Herald*.

Brown, R. (2008, September). Sustainability: Being fashionably fashionable. *Management*, p. 69.

Campbell, G. (2005, April 9-15). So hot! *New Zealand Listener*, 198 / 3387.

Daniell, S. (2007, May 5-11). Woman of the cloth. *New Zealand Listener*.

Department for Environment, Food and Rural Affairs (Defra) (2007). Mapping of evidence on sustainable development impacts that occur in the life cycle of clothing. http://randd.defra.gov.uk/Document.aspx?Document=EV02028_7073_FRP.pdf Accessed 1 May 2010.

Department of Conservation (2008). Threats and impacts: Possums. www.doc.govt.nz/templates/podcover.aspx?id=33422 Accessed 10 March 2008.

EarthPositive (2008). Climate neutral apparel. www.earthpositiveonline.com Accessed 5 February 2008.

Fashion Industry New Zealand (2005a, May). The chain gang: Australian and New Zealand apparel. www.finz.co.nz/media.php Accessed 26 June 2007.

Fashion Industry New Zealand (2005b, August). Contemplating the issues: Australian and New Zealand apparel. www.finz.co.nz/media.php Accessed 26 June 2007.

Fashion Industry New Zealand (2007, May 25). Feature: Stuck in the middle with you. www.finz.co.nz/news Accessed 26 June 2007.

Hume, M. (2012, April 26). What hope have local brands got of fighting back? Renowned fashion editor Marion Hume talks tough with fashion executives at an Inforum Group lunch in Sydney. Fashion Industry New Zealand http://www.finz.co.nz/default.aspx?TabID=36207&category=Resources Accessed 19 April 2013.

Kim, N. (21 November 2007). Green is the new black for savvy consumers, Retailers. Reuters, www.news.yahoo.com Accessed 22 November 2007.

Linda Loudermilk. (2007). Linda Loudermilk: About www.lindaloudermilk.com/loudermilkinc.html Accessed 23 October 2007.

Moon, J. (2008). Sustainability: Icebreaker. *Mindfood.com*, p. 107.

New Zealand Retailers Association (2012). The retail market in New Zealand: An analysis 2011/12. http://www.retail.org.nz/downloads/2011-12%20Retail%20Market%20in%20NZ%20-April%202012%20Final%20version.pdf Accessed 20 April 2013.

New Zealand Trade and Enterprise. (2004). Fashioning distinctive style. *Bright*, Issue 07, pp. 16-19.

Oliver, A. (2012, May 9). Style briefs—Free the Sea. *Christchurch Press*. http://www.stuff.co.nz/the-press/christchurch-life/zest/6884897/Style-briefs-May-9

Starfish (2013). About Starfish, Our clothes. http://www.starfish.co.nz/about/our-clothes Accessed 21 April 2013.

Sustainable Business Network (2011). Sustainable fashion means connecting with nature. A SBN case study on Miranda Brown Conscious Cloth http://sustainable.org.nz/cms/uploads/2011%20Awards/Northern/Miranda%20Brown%20Case%20Study%20-%20Final%20and%20Signed%20Off.pdf Accessed 20 April 2013.

The Economist (2008, March 1). Kiwis on the catwalk: The unlikely rise of New Zealand's fashion industry. *The Economist*, p. 64.

Thomas, D. (2007). Deluxe: How luxury lost its lustre. London: Penguin.

Unterberger, L. (2007). Eco chic fashion: Green pieces. www.slideshow.ivillage.com/igo_green Accessed 26 June 2007.

Untouched World New Zealand. (2007). Vision. www.untouchedworld.com/en/uw/vision.htm Accessed 19 October 2007.

West, L. (2007). Top fashion designers turn eco-friendly fabrics into haute couture. www.environmentabout.com/od/earthtalkcolumns/a/ecofashion.htm. Accessed 22 October 2007.

About the Journal of Corporate Citizenship

THE JOURNAL OF CORPORATE CITIZENSHIP (*JCC*) is a multidisciplinary peer-reviewed journal that focuses on integrating theory about corporate citizenship with management practice. It provides a forum in which the tensions and practical realities of making corporate citizenship real can be addressed in a reader-friendly, yet conceptually and empirically rigorous format.

JCC aims to publish *the best ideas integrating the theory and practice of corporate citizenship in a format that is readable, accessible, engaging, interesting and useful* for readers in its already wide audience in business, consultancy, government, NGOs and academia. It encourages practical, theoretically sound, and (when relevant) empirically rigorous manuscripts that address real-world implications of corporate citizenship in global and local contexts. Topics related to corporate citizenship can include (but are not limited to): corporate responsibility, stakeholder relationships, public policy, sustainability and environment, human and labour rights/issues, governance, accountability and transparency, globalisation, small and medium-sized enterprises (SMEs) as well as multinational firms, ethics, measurement, and specific issues related to corporate citizenship, such as diversity, poverty, education, information, trust, supply chain management, and problematic or constructive corporate/human behaviours and practices.

In addition to articles linking the theory and practice of corporate citizenship, *JCC* also encourages innovative or creative submissions (for peer review). Innovative submissions can highlight issues of corporate citizenship from a critical perspective, enhance practical or conceptual understanding of corporate citizenship, or provide new insights or alternative perspectives on the realities of corporate citizenship in today's world. Innovative submissions might include: critical perspectives and controversies, photography, essays, poetry, drama, reflections, and other innovations that help bring corporate citizenship to life for management practitioners and academics alike.

JCC welcomes contributions from researchers and practitioners involved in any of the areas mentioned above. Manuscripts should be written so that they are comprehensible to an intelligent reader, avoiding jargon, formulas and extensive methodological treatises wherever possible. They should use examples and illustrations to highlight the ideas, concepts and practical implications of the ideas being presented. Theory is important and necessary; but theory—with the empirical research and conceptual work that supports theory—needs to be balanced by integration into practices to stand the tests of time and usefulness. *JCC* aims to be the premier journal to publish articles on corporate citizenship that accomplish this integration of theory and practice. We want the journal to be read as much by executives leading corporate citizenship as it is by academics seeking sound research and scholarship.

JCC appears quarterly and includes peer-reviewed papers by leading writers, with occasional reviews, case studies and think-pieces. A key feature is the 'Turning Points' section. Turning Points are commentaries, controversies, new ideas, essays and insights that aim to be provocative and engaging, raise the important issues of the day and provide observations on what is too new yet to be the subject of empirical and theoretical studies. *JCC* continues to produce occasional issues dedicated to a single theme. These have included 'Story-telling: Beyond the Academic Article—Using Fiction, Art and Literary Techniques to Communicate', 'Sustainable Luxury', 'Business–NGO Partnerships', 'Creating Global Citizens and Responsible Leadership', 'Responsible Investment in Emerging Markets', 'The Positive Psychology of Sustainable Enterprise', 'Textiles, Fashion and Sustainability', 'Designing Management Education', 'Managing by Design' and 'Innovative Stakeholder.

EDITORS

General Editor:

Professor Malcolm McIntosh, Bath Spa University, UK; email: jcc@greenleaf-publishing.com

Regional Editor:

North American Editor: Sandra Waddock, Professor of Management, Boston College, Carroll School of Management, Senior Research Fellow, Center for Corporate Citizenship, Chestnut Hill, MA 02467 USA; tel: +1 617 552 0477; fax: +1 617 552 0433; email: waddock@bc.edu

Notes for Contributors

SUBMISSIONS

All content should be submitted via online submission. For more information see the journal homepage at www.greenlea publishing.com/jcc.

The form gives prompts for the required information and asks authors to submit the full text of the paper, including the tit author name and author affiliation, as a Word attachment. **Abstract and keywords will be completed via the online submissic and are not necessary on the attachment.**

As part of the online submission authors will be asked to tick a box to state they have read and adhere to the Greenleaf–GS Copyright Guidelines and have permission to publish the paper, including all figures, images, etc which have been taken fro: other sources. It is the author's responsibility to ensure this is correct.

In order to be able to distribute papers published in Greenleaf journals, we need signed transfer of copyright from the author We are committed to a liberal and fair approach to copyright and accessibility, and do not restrict authors' rights to reuse the own work for personal use or in an institutional repository.

A brief autobiographical note should be supplied at the end of the paper including:

- Full name
- Affiliation
- Email address
- Full international contact details

Please supply (via online submission) an **abstract outlining the title, purpose, methodology and main findings**. It's wor considering that, as your paper will be located and read online, the quality of your abstract will determine whether readers go c to access your full paper. We recommend you place particular focus on the impact of your research on further research, practi or society. What does your paper contribute?

In addition, please provide up to **six descriptive keywords**.

FORMATTING YOUR PAPER

Headings should be short and in bold text, with a clear and consistent hierarchy.

Please identify **Notes or Endnotes** with consecutive numbers, enclosed in square brackets and listed at the end of the article.

Figures and other images should be submitted as .jpeg (.jpg) or .tif files and be of a high quality. Please number consecutive with Arabic numerals and mark clearly within the body of the text where they should be placed.

If images are not the original work of the author, it is the author's responsibility to obtain written consent from the copyrig holder to them being used. Authors will be asked to confirm this is the case by ticking the box on the online submission to sa they have read and understood the Greenleaf–GSE copyright policy. Images which are neither the authors' own work, nor a accompanied by such permission will not be published.

Tables should be included as part of the manuscript, with relevant captions.

Supplementary data can be appended to the article, using the form and should follow the same formatting rules as the mai text.

References to other publications should be complete and in Harvard style, e.g. (Jones, 2011) for one author, (Jones and Smit. 2011) for two authors and (Jones *et al.*, 2011) for more than two authors. A full reference list should appear at the end of th paper.

- For **books**: Surname, Initials (year), *Title of Book*, Publisher, Place of publication.
  e.g. Author, J. (2011), *This is my book*, Publisher, New York, NY.
- For **book chapters**: Surname, Initials (year), "Chapter title", Editor's Surname, Initials, *Title of Book*, Publisher, Place o publication, pages (if known).
- For **journals**: Surname, Initials (year), "Title of article", *Title of Journal*, volume, number, pages.
- For **conference proceedings**: Surname, Initials (year), "Title of paper", in Surname, Initials (Ed.), Title of published proceeding which may include place and date(s) held, Publisher, Place of publication, Page numbers.
- For **newspaper articles**: Surname, Initials (year) (if an author is named), "Article title", *Newspaper*, date, pages.
- For **images**:
  Where image is from a printed source—as for books but with the page number on which the image appears.
  Where image is from an online source—Surname, Initials (year), Title, Available at, Date accessed.
  Other images—Surname, Initials (year), Title, Name of owner (person or institution) and location for viewing.

▶ **To discuss ideas for contributions**, please contact the General Editor: Professor Malcolm McIntosh, Bath Spa University, U email: jcc@greenleaf-publishing.com.

For Product Safety Concerns and Information please contact our EU
representative GPSR@taylorandfrancis.com Taylor & Francis Verlag GmbH,
Kaufingerstraße 24, 80331 München, Germany

Printed and bound by CPI Group (UK) Ltd, Croydon, CR0 4YY

08/05/2025

01864511-0009